Endless Transition

Eight transitional life lessons on how to overcome infinite change, career shifts, & triumphant failures.

A Veteran's memoir

Part Two

Air Force Master Sergeant
William C. Gonzalez

Table of Contents

Preface

Before we start any journey, we start by asking questions....am I ready...can I do this...what will happen to me...can I make it...do they want me...why me...why not... why the fuck...how.....who did this....why does this keep happening? Every emotion you've ever felt as a transitioning veteran or civilian who had to drop everything to start over will be expressed in this book. My journey is similar to others.....no the fuck it isn't. Mistake number one is trying to make your experiences match those of everyone else's. I am special and so are you.

We are not meant to be like other people. There is not a happy homogeneous tribe of successful bowling pins for us to emulate. Be fucking proud to be unique. Be proud to struggle. And never run from a challenge. Never Ever run from a challenge. Look that damn challenge right in the damn face and tell it "you won't fucking break me". All my life I've had many (too fucking many) instances of the world trying to snap my ass in half. It almost got close to breaking me in too.....but being extremely flexible made that impossible. I can break, but when I choose to break on my terms. The fight is endless, and the sooner you realize that, the better you will be equipped to fight back every damn day of your life. The hits will never stop coming until you break and let that furry bastard know it's over. Saying "I Quit" is allowing stress to manifest as an actual being. What you may read within this memoir may shock you, and I hope it does and you never make the same mistakes I have.

Be better than me and better than yourself, because you are a warrior. Live every day knowing that time is relative to your perception of it. Take time back and never stop being ready for the onslaught of struggle. Regardless of where you come from, your hard times can be felt by normal people everywhere. I am just like you. I am an African-American who grew up in the hard city of the Bronx NY, I came from humble beginnings and nothing was ever given to me for free. I earned everything I've accomplished from my military decorations to college degrees, hard work does pay off! These are tough times. Let's get through this together.

This memoir serves as an insight into my life and the events that have shaped me into the man I have grown to become. The stories and the overall journey I embarked on from early childhood to my mid 30's are all 100% true and without any level of fabrication. I am reminded daily, that not everyone is fortunate enough to have lived my life (both for the good and the bad). For this, it was my duty to ensure those who may be transitioning have the guidance to make better decisions than those who step through the door before them.

The COVID-19 Pandemic has reminded the world not to get too comfortable as things can change in an instant. Do we have the tools to survive that next change in our lives? I hope you enjoy my memoir and spread the lessons you read with others so that we can thrive and remain prosperous in our future endeavors. I have been told by close friends and family members that this memoir can be emotionally taxing and must be read in increments. Read, learn, and absorb at your own pace.

First Transition:

From Peace to War - The Spark of Unknown Origins

I knew exactly where I was and how I felt when 9/11 occurred all over America. Shit, that was the most fucked up way to start my senior year of high school. Sitting in jazz band class and reviewing the last few musical notes of the song we were about to play, one of our band teachers informed the class that a plane had flown into the World Trade Center. I am 18 at this time and have never lived through such an event to understand or assume what the hell was really happening. In fact, I assumed some dumb ass pilot flying a small ass plane ran straight into those giant buildings that can be seen for miles. "How the fuck did a plane hit the WTC?" I was very naive at this time and absolutely had no idea what was happening outside my school on the southern tip of Manhattan.

As we ended class early and headed to our home rooms, we received the word that another plane had hit the towers. Again, I have no historical reference as to the severity of such an event and said to myself "did that same motherfucker hit the tower again? Dumb ass pilot." Skip a few hours and we are now scared shitless because we were told by our teachers what was happening just 7 miles away to the south of us. I have one vivid memory of one of my teachers pacing back and forth and in the classroom with her hands behind her back like some war General giving a briefing to soldiers about to enter battle. "We are at war class.....if you don't believe it, there will be fighter jets and tanks rolling through the streets here soon." What kind of General Patton shit was she trying to pull off? I mean, of course we're a class full of hardened New York kids, but fuck this kind of talk! We are not built for this. It would become clearer to me that of all the kids in the world, New York City kids are exactly built and bred for this kind of conflict. Conflict in the form of not having a stable home, worrying about wearing the wrong colors during gang initiation week, wondering if your father will beat you because he's had too much to drink, worrying if that shot you heard in the street is coming your way.

War was coming, but imagine that you're old enough to fight in it. I've watched tons of movies about military conflict and enjoyed it for the entertainment & historical value, but I never looked deeper into the stories of war and how it scares good men and women for life. Watching Saving Private Ryan (1998) for the first time in the theaters, when It was released, was the SCARIEST film I've ever watched. During the opening scene, the Omaha Beach landing, I started to tremble and shake uncontrollably. Unknown to me, this was fear that I would feel again later in life during my second combat deployment to Afghanistan in support of Operations Enduring Freedom. I was afraid......no I was terrified of that movie because it actually happened to men and women who were no older than I was at the time I watched the film. Men and Women of

World War II lived, fought, and died through those events that were so vividly depicted through the motion pictures and the sound......the grueling sounds of combat, pain, and people begging for their mother with the guts hanging out. Would I have the courage to do such a thing if called upon to do so?

I looked out the classroom window during our lockdown at the school and noticed an ever growing line of people across the street. If you start from the back of the line and work your way forward towards the front, you'll find that it ends and at the blood bank & donation center for the American Red Cross. This was the first scene I witnessed that sparked the unknown love that I have for America. A scene that was both beautiful and dramatically somber at the same time. The feeling of both sadness and anger conflicted within my soul to produce an overwhelming feeling of helplessness and the need for vengeance. Myself and the other students were released from school and were told to go straight home. From 68th street in Manhattan to 167th street in The Bronx is exactly 7.1 miles of walking.

During my walk from school, I periodically turned my head and body to look back south at the dust cloud from the carnage. The walk took about two hours for me to complete which left me with nothing but time to think and mostly, reflect. How can I help? Did anyone die down there? Of course they did...what a dumb questions. Will this happen again? Oh shit this could happen again....what will we do? Who could have done this? At this point during the walk and the many questions I asked myself, I have not seen the footage of the actual planes hitting the building and didn't know that the World Trade Centers had fallen; eliminating them from the New York skyline. Really, what the hell was happening today?

What am I supposed to do, and why do I feel like I'm supposed to do something? I want to do something. I need to do something. Patriotism is the sleeping giant inside every American. But unfortunately, It takes an extraordinary event to bring out this uncontrollable beast, filled with pride, anger, compassion, and empathy towards the ideals of America. I would later choose to join the United States Air Force during my senior year of high school after much deliberation with myself.

The choice though was not mine to make, but rather it was made for me. How so you ask? Allow me to explain...I was walking in the Bronx on Tremont Ave two days after 9/11 going to visit my grandmother. While walking down the street, I heard the roar of an Aircraft above me. This roar was not the usual sound emitted from the aircraft leaving LaGuardia, Newark, or JFK Airport. It was different, powerful, soft & dangerous at the same time. It was an F-16 Fighting Falcon jet plane. I've only seen those aircraft in the movies and pictures up till this point in my young life. Now, it was flying right over my neighborhood and over my head. I knew at that very moment, that's where I wanted to be and what I wanted to be a part of. But no "why did I join the military" story is complete without a funny moment of Zen. Here goes...

As I left my school with a new sense of purpose and boldness, I received the letter from the government that is sent to all men to fill out the Selective Service form. Once you turn 18, the government knows about it, and they are going to get service time from your ass come hell or high water. Shit, at that time I was more than happy to fill out the card that tells the government (and recruiters) you are open for military business. I selected the Air Force as my service branch of interest and placed it back in the mail as soon as possible. Not knowing at all how the process worked, I expected the recruiters to be knocking down my door trying to recruit me. One day, I received a telephone call from a military recruiter. Let's call this recruiter Sergeant (Sgt) Murray. Sergeant Murray asked to speak to William Gonzalez..."speaking, how can I help you?"

He introduced himself and informed me that he got wind of me wanting to join the service. Mind you, Sergeant Murray is an Army recruiter. Not sure how he even got my phone number. I told the Army recruiter "I was really interested in joining the Air Force. This motherfucka told me "oh yea, we can help you with that." Me not knowing anything about military service or recruitment, how the fuck was I supposed to know this numb nut can't do shit for me joining the US Air Force. But of course I didn't know shit, and assumed Sgt Murray could've helped me with my career goals. Now I have always considered myself an individual who always wanted more training and never hid away from an opportunity to make myself better. This was absolutely a missed moment of progressive enhancement in my life. As funny as it was, I'm definitely not proud of this moment. I actually ended the phone call believing this Army recruiter can help me enter the Air Force....why why why did I believe such a thing? I set the appointment on my mental calendar and prepared to see the Army recruiter who could help me join the Air Force. On that day, I headed down to Third Avenue in the Bronx where the recruiting office was. I truly believe in the concept of fate because of this moment in my life. I Learned If it isn't meant for you now, it isn't meant for you later! I arrived at the building, labeled in manner of Army this, Army that, Army Here, there, fucking green eggs and ham everywhere. Again, why did I walk in?

So I walked in.........with the hopes of receiving help joining the US Air Force (insert joke here). I'm greeted by a foaming sea of green, light green, and dark green of both men and women in uniform. I met Sgt Murray who greets me kindly. Small talk ensues as I dance around the nagging thought in my head, "I have a strong feeling these guys are not going to help me join the Air Force."

During initial consideration, it is important to understand the military won't even consider you if you are too overweight or can't pass the aptitude test. But before you take the actual aptitude test to qualify for entrance into the US military, you'll always receive a practice test. Lucky for me......I love tests, right? No....no I do not love taking tests. I was sat down by the recruiter and given the practice test to enter the US Army. This test isn't anything too difficult, maybe 25 to 40 questions of an assortment of topics from mechanical engineering to administrative functions. I took the test.....finished the test....and handed it back to Sgt Murray. The minimum passing score for that damn test was 30.....30 I tell ya, 30! What did I receive......a phenomenal 29.000!

Holy shit, I bombed the US Army's practice test! Sgt Murray saw my score and proceeded to politely tell me to get the fuck out of his office and come back when I can meet the bottom standard. This was the best failure of my life because it turns out, believe it or not, Army recruiters can't get you into the Air Force. Who knew! After I untucked myself from between my ass, I proceeded to contact the Air Force recruiter, who by the way...almost wanted nothing to do with me. I took the pre-test and passed it just fine. I was now on my way to becoming an Airman and supporting the first war of my adult life. I couldn't be more proud of what I was about to do. Graduating high school was the first step in my first transition from teenager to adult, to military professional. My last year of high school, with the events of 9/11 in the background, was filled with mixed emotion and too many relationships that I had to break away from.

Although normal, high school was the least of my worries when it comes to this transitional period. With my high school graduation completed, I enjoyed one more month of summer as a civilian. My last summer seeing the sites of the city I learned to love as a child and learned to also deeply hate. I was both excited and a little anxious of the unknowns of my future career. I was joining the Air Force initially as a Loadmaster, which is an aviation position flying aboard military cargo aircraft. To keep this part of my life as no surprise, I did not become a Loadmaster in the Air Force. Why didn't I.......let's go back to the Military Entrance Processing Station (MEPS) where I learned that the military was no joke to laugh at.

We arrived in Brooklyn, Fort Hamilton at 0500 (5 AM). We wait outside for someone to let us in the MEPS building and tell us what to do. MEPS is a very simple process where all you are expected to do is follow instructions. Standing in line to be told the next station to enter was the easiest process of MEPS. I initially wanted to be a Security Forces Airman (military police). The reason for that career choice was simple, I wanted a career where I used a firearm regularly. I joined during a time of war and fully expected to be thrusted into the fires of combat. Here's why that did not happen. Being a Bronx kid has proved to me that public knowledge is not so public. When I took my eye exam at the MEPS' various medical stations, I had to take the depth perception test which evaluated your ability to identify items that are either close or far away. The test uses circles in a row (usually five) with one of the circles being manipulated to visually appear closer. As simple as this test sounds, I failed because I couldn't discern the 3-dimensional differences between the circles. My dreams of becoming a Security Forces airman were eliminated because it's hard to justify placing a candidate into a career where deadly force may be used if they can't tell how far the target is.

Later in the process, which took an entire day, military personnel forced every candidate to read a particular law from the Uniform Code of Military Justice. Article 85 of the Uniform Code of Military Justice details the punishment for service members found guilty of Desertion. The Article states: "Any person found guilty of desertion or attempt to desert shall be punished, if the offense is committed in time of war, by death or such other punishment as a court-martial may direct, but if the desertion or attempt to desert occurs at any other time, by such punishment, other than death, as a court-martial may direct." This was eye opening to read because that meant anyone who runs away during time of war, can be killed if and when caught. My second unofficial transition began from curious teenager, to committed adult.I knew this profession could get me killed…..and I'm ok with that reality. So I can't be a cop in the Air Force because I failed the depth perception test (not based on visual acuity, but lack of knowledge).

What's next? What profession can I do that would guarantee that I see some form of combat in response to the terrorist attacks of September 11th? I spoke to the in-house recruiter at MEPS who asks "is there anything else you'd like to do?" My simple answer, as with every answer I choose to give…..whatever job I can do that allows me to regularly carry a weapon. This was the best and worst answer I can give because recruiters don't care about what the candidate wants.

It's about what jobs are needed to be filled and how they can fill them. My scores were not great but I was able to be talked into signing a contract for a Loadmaster job. Now, if you are unfamiliar, a Loadmaster is a military specialty in the Air Force that loads, secures, transports both cargo and passengers on Air Force cargo aircraft.

This is an aviation position that flies in combat support aircraft. This is NOT a combat job that will get me into the shit I hoped to be in. But I didn't know that fact at the time, and the recruiter didn't care to elaborate on the difference between combat and combat support. He needed to get this job filled and I was here waving my hand to "send me." Oh yes, he sent me alright! I signed the contract and entered the United State Air Force ready and willing to fight or die for my country as a......LOADMASTER! Merica, sarcasm level 9000!

I was proud to have the opportunity to serve my county in it's time of need in any capacity. So honestly, it didn't matter what job they gave me....I was on my way. I left New York City for Basic Training on 13 August 2002. Air Force Basic Training at the time was held at San Antonio Texas and was six weeks long (or rather six weeks short). Basic Training provided me with the intense experience of having my whole world turned upside down by letting me know I had limited control over my actions. Completing Basic was the best feeling I ever had up to that point in my life. It was the feeling of graduating military training during a time of war and that was special, because only about 2% of all Americans at this time were in the military. This non-drafted, all volunteer force made up the entirety of the US Military during the Global War on Terrorism. I started my Technical Training at the Aircrew Fundamentals course which taught the absolute basics of Aircrew duties and responsibilities. At this course, we as students are provided with a little more information about the specific aviation career field we chose.

To my surprise, I learned through my diligent academic studies that Loadmasters.......don't see much combat. Hum, imagine that... I was duped into a job that I knew nothing about in order to satisfy a quota. It goes without saying that once I knew this truth (I would be hauling cargo or bullets around for the ones that are doing the actual fighting) I immediately opted out of the course. Since aviation service is 100% voluntary, members can choose to drop during initial training. My Instructor looked at me like I was an idiot. He only saw the loss of per diem, travel time, flying, and many other perks associated with flying. I didn't care about any of that. I just wanted to fight. My instructor asked "well hell, what do you want to do?" "Security Forces" I replied.

After a brief moment of internal laughter followed by an overt "the fuck for" by my instructor, I defended my choice and continued with my academic withdrawal from flying training. I was officially dropped and sent into academic limbo. I visited the personnel office and filled out my career selection form in which I identified Security Forces as my top pick. The personalist informs me that I have to pass the depth perception test (my natural nemesis). It's not going to beat me this time, because now I know what the hell they are talking about. I was ready for this test and the opening of new doors. I proceeded to the medical office and took my eye exam.

Glory Glory Glory I passed the test and could tell that one of those damn circles did not look like the others. Since that was the only requirement I needed to be considered for Security Forces duty, I was sure to get the job I wanted...right? Hell No! Why would you ever think that will be my reality. It's ok my friend (I say to myself internally) you will learn this lesson over and over again. So which job was I awarded (drum roll please)? I'll give you a hint, it's not what I wanted. I was on my way to becoming a bonafide Logistics Planner. "The fuck is that" is what I asked myself until I started my training every day and night.

To recount, within the first 3 months of my military career, I rode an emotional rollercoaster in which I prepared for and was removed from two careers. I experienced disappointment and confusion as early as 19 years old. How was I prepared to move from job to job and keep moving forward? The answer was simple. The same way I moved forward during my childhood in which I was moved from foster home to foster home because me and my siblings were children of the system. A system that was meant to protect us against parents who had substance abuse issues. I was born in 1983....crack cocaine was running ramped in my family and caused us to be taken from our mother for our protection (or so they said). Let me share my story on how I grew up living with my mother, grandmother, 5 foster mothers and my father before leaving to join the US Air Force in 2002.

Alpha Transition

The decisions you make to change your life, career, friendships, or location in order to better yourself are in your best interest. Stick by your choice! I assure you, the road will be filled with barriers that were created to stop you in your tracks. Be the boulder that destroys anything in front of you. Approach the choice you've made with conviction and grit. It doesn't matter if you are unsure of the future, and it doesn't matter if you are perfectly prepared for it...own your inevitable struggle! It is always easier to choose the path of least resistance. Take a look at the greatest people in history. I'm not here to give you names or examples...you know who that person or persons are. Look at their life and find that person's struggle.

The tough times are what will define you for the longevity of your adult life. Be proud of your decisions and remove anyone or anything that does not support your journey. The mistake that is often made is not trusting yourself. Have confidence, even when the plan is not perfect. We as a species and society become more intelligent by solving complex problems. Do not deny yourself the opportunity to learn and retain the knowledge that will help you survive this harsh environment. Be the boulder, and never stop asking questions when things are not clear. Figure it out at all costs! Transitioning successfully at all levels is based on your ability to survive and operate. This world needs you, you must survive this trial, for it will make you stronger.

Transition Two:

From Nature to Nurture - <u>What does family look like</u>?

There is no easy way to say this, but the raw truth of my childhood was not worth celebrating. I didn't grow up with perfect memories of a mother who raised me and my siblings with a loving father who taught me how to be a man. Nor did I have the experience of a child who was supported by loving parents for what he wished to do in the future. In fact my childhood was the direct opposite. There was very little support provided to me and my sisters and brothers in the early 80's, which led to traumatic experiences that shape our lives still to this day. Just two days ago while sitting with my older sister, I held her hand to console the tears from her eyes as she told me "I feel like I'm cursed because I look the most like mommy." Simply looking like our mother or any of our parents may be a determinant trait of bad luck in our future.

Why did we deserve such persistent pain that was still felt by us as lost adult children in our late 30's. We have kids of our own and careers that we are currently pursuing, but every day we realized our childhood provided us with shocking instability that led to anger, depression, isolation, and the feeling of dread towards our unclear future. The choice to be successful was a deliberate uphill struggle with a 500 lbs. book bag on our backs. Myself and my siblings were born between

1971 and 1993. New York City (especially in the Bronx) was a breeding ground for violence, drug use, and burning buildings everywhere for as far as the eyes can see. As children, me and my sisters (before my brothers were born) would always go outside to play in the neighborhood, mostly unattended at the ages of 4 - 7 years old. We would do everything together from playing tag, hide and seek in the park, to playing man-hunt in adjacent vacant buildings with other neighborhood friends and cousins. Sometimes, we would look into the burned wreckage of buildings in our neighborhood that were never repaired or removed until years later, wondering what life might have been like for those who lived there; did they die here, is their spirits still present? We would also take unnecessary risk & chance of getting in trouble every summer by sneaking into the public pool after dark when it was closed. Specifically, Crotona Pool (inside of Crotona Park) was not heavily reinforced from a break-in perspective as it is today. It was an inviting area for children and adults to relax and escape the perils of the Bronx streets; and for a small glimpse of time, be at peace.

Every night during the summer, we as children (no older than 7) would walk through the park to squeeze our little bodies (that were remarkably flexible and nibble) through the bars of the fence to sneak into the pool and the shower area. This was particularly foolish because none of us were good swimmers. We never received formal instruction from anyone on how to survive in the water supervised or unsupervised. In fact, we didn't know how to swim with any technique or simply tread water deeper than 3 ½ feet. The pools were left ON overnight for filtration and cleaning for public use the next day, which was more of a tempting reason we opted to enter the pool against the rules....it looked beautiful to us. In fact the entire facility was left operational allowing us kids to run into and out of the shower rooms, turn on all the showers and run up and down the bathrooms with not one to yell at us or tell us to stop what we were doing. We would run (always running because our time was limited as we always assumed the police were not far behind) back to the pool to swim in the 1 - 4 feet pool while trying to be as quiet as possible. But everyone in the neighborhood knew we were in there. Hell they probably just left after sneaking in themselves.

But we were kids, children, adolescents. We didn't know how to be quiet, and why should we, we were bored and having a great time breaking and entering. So once the neighborhood noticed all the noise we were making to the point that it started to disturb their peace, they decided to call the cops. Once the police showed up at the pool, me and my sisters & cousins would scatter out of the pool area like roaches in light; run back through the gates, and disappeared like ghosts through the park. On one occasion, me and my sisters were off playing in an abandoned lot that had been temporarily made into a landfill by the community. Meaning, the town threw all it's garbage all over the place.

This empty lot used to be the foundation for a residential building, but like many buildings in the Bronx from the 1970's - 80's it had burned down during the blazing fires of the 1970's. People would throw away all kinds of garbage, old beds, and sometimes toys that we would clean and take home for our own entertainment. So me and the Sister Gang would walk through the block-sized lot in search of something cool. On this night, we were extra bored and didn't have anything to do or anywhere to go. One of my sisters had a box of matches with her from god knows where. So as most kids would do when met with the obstacle of boredom, we decided to light a few items of trash on fire. What we burned exactly escapes my memory, but I'll never forget the feeling we all had when the fire got bigger.....and Bigger......and BIGGER. The flame continued to grow until we realized "oh shit, it's not going out." We were the kids in the neighborhood who had been largely unsupervised for years. No one had taught us that you can extinguish a fire with dirt in the absence of water, so we watched it burn. Then......

We fucking panicked and ran to call the Fire Department from the Red Box (no not the one with movies). Back in the day, every city block had a built-in Fire/Police call box. Once you pressed the button (with the fear of God on the back of your neck), it dialed the respective dispatch for that agency you are trying to reach. A red button for the Fire Department, and a blue button for the Police Department. We began running away from the burning blaze that is surrounded by more garbage to find the nearest call box. We arrived and pressed the red button, the operator answered.

My oldest sister tells the operator there's a fire burning in our neighborhood. Even as the operator answered, we knew not to speak too much because the operator would be able to find out who we were and send us to jail. This is what kids in our era thought about constantly; that we were always one foot away from being sent to jail. The box location is transmitted and a fire truck is dispatched to the vacant lot to fight the blaze we carelessly set. Since we lived across the street from the fire which we started, our home provided a quick retreat to watch the rapid fire response. The commonality of the stories we shared from our childhood was the lack of parental supervision.

Our mother, who I love dearly, was a user of crack-cocaine, alcohol, and other substances I may not have been aware of. I knew there was a heavy use of illegal substances within my family and within our household because of the little blue, red, or yellow top crack vials I would see in front of our home as we returned home from elementary school. It is not fair to suggest that my family and upbringing was unique in any way. In fact, it was not very different from the lives of thousands of families in New York City at that time. Most of my cousins and the other neighborhood kids (especially those of African American descent) were affected by the same lack of supervision me and my sisters experienced. Even as a teenager, I've unfortunately witnessed my older cousin (who later died of a heroin overdose) shoot up heroin in the middle of the night as he slept in the bed close to mine (separated by only a satin curtain).

I knew my cousin was using because of his strange behavior throughout the day and the light of his lighter in the middle of the night which he used to heat up his narcotic solution. I knew what he was doing, but this was the life I'd been dealt.

Suffer in silence was a phrase I learned years before the military. With the wide-spread use of crack and fatherless homes, kids were left alone often and were observed/supervised by police, teachers, or other neighbors.

There were plenty of people who witnessed myself and my sisters out and about in the neighborhoods and reported us to the authorities. Whether it was recognizing us fleeing from the police from the public pool, or asking our Puerto Rican neighbor for food because we were hungry; our mother was not home, the journey into foster care was assured. There have been years of neglect for me and my siblings as children that led to us being able to see most of the Bronx in a way that you wouldn't expect of children that were less than 10 years old. Indeed, I have lived through many events which shaped my way of thinking as an adult. We were dirty kids...I was a dirty kid. I played in the dirt all the time and had very little assistance from our mother and my father because they were not there...never around when it mattered. My father worked and lived in a separate apartment from my mother. To ensure the facts are clear, my father was just MY father. I didn't share the same father with my other sisters and brothers, nor did they with me. If I were to count, I have one mother, and 5 different men with the title of father in the maternal sense only. For years I thought this was normal, kids in New York City always had fathers that were never there or families had multiple fathers assigned.

With our parents not very present, we became filthy from always playing outside. Which led to us becoming sick and contracting serious and infectious diseases. One of the diseases and conditions I contracted from playing outside and in the filth was Scabies. This sounds like something that is cute and tolerable, but I assure it's not. Scabies is a rash that I contracted on my legs (mostly my thighs) that spread to about 40 percent of my leg. It was the itchiest and uncomfortable rash I have ever had in my life. I remember the burning sensation I would feel every day when I woke up and every night before I went to sleep.

I remember while looking at my leg, which would flex due to the regular movement of being a child, I would always visually capture the cracks of red which looked like a river of blood running across my thighs. Scabies weren't just a bad rash, it was the borrowing of mites under my skin which caused intense itching and scabbing from broken skin for about 3 weeks. I was never treated medically for scabies in a medical institution, and my mother never knew about it. I assumed it was something naturally occurring in nature that would go away so long as I washed properly. Even before contracting scabies, me and my sisters had already been in and out of foster homes all over New York City. Every child who grew up in foster care can remember a few things about their experiences. We all knew who our social workers were and the child care agency they worked for. I can't recall the names of my social worker, but I remember his face as he became a prominent figure in our life. We saw him all the time during supervised visitations with our mother and family one weekend a month. We would always have our social worker pick us up to see our family during Family Court hearings, and have them drop us off when it was finished. Sometimes, those rides back to the foster home were filled with our social worker attempting to reassure us that it will get better, our mother needs more time, we'll try again at the next hearing.

The agency he worked for was called Little Flower Children and Family Services. We knew everything about the system and how it worked, or so we thought we did. We even thought we knew how the family justice system worked in our favor or against us. As kids, we thought the legal system was actively trying to keep our family apart. Of course, we didn't know anything about how the justice system actually operated. We never knew if our mother was drug tested during our foster care to ensure she was sober & clean enough to care for us. We didn't realize the system was trying to protect us from the environment of drug use and potential physical abuse that we were party to. We didn't know that the lawyers assigned to us were never out to keep our family apart. We as children learned to love and hate at an early age. And I can tell you honestly, we had hate in our hearts for the lawyer that represented the State of NY. Her name was Vicki. We thought she was the worst person in the world because as kids, she was the one in court telling that judge that our mom failed that drug test, that our mom was not ready to parent, that our mother did not have any stable income, that our mom could not take care of us. We were always angry at Vicki for telling the judge those things because we knew it would keep us in foster care longer. Why would she say whose things all the time in court?

We just wanted to go home and didn't care what our mother was up to...so long as we could not be in foster care anymore. We missed our mother so bad that it would hurt us to go to sleep. Court visits were always hard on me and my siblings because it served as both a joyous occasion where we could see our real family, but turned sad when we would not receive a positive verdict and were forced to leave our family again. Leaving was hard on me and my siblings because we cried a lot as we left and were placed back into the van and returned to foster care. I don't remember the first time we were sent to foster care or the reason why. I think I was about 4 or 5 years old when we were sent to different places to live with people we didn't know. What I remember the most was the feeling of not being truly loved the way a child feels from their parents.

These people volunteered to care for us, for which I am grateful, but the love felt within the naturalized family was never there. I remember living in a brownstone house in Brooklyn with a very nice African-American couple we stayed with for a short while. Time was not properly measured for us as children. I didn't wear watches or had a phone to reference when I needed to know what day it was. I don't know how long we lived in that brownstone in Brooklyn, but I remember sleeping in a large bed with my sisters next to a pet tarantula that was kept in the same room as us. I never knew why they had a pet tarantula in that house, but why in the hell would you have the kids sleep in the same room as it? Every night that damn tarantula would try to escape its habitat, making a ton of noise as we slept next to it. I couldn't describe a more horrifying nightmare for kids from the Bronx who learned to be scared of Water Bugs (Giant Cockroaches) that crawled up and down our kitchens. We would scream every night by screaming out for the names of our foster parents to save us.

They would respond annoyed that we woke them up claiming the spider can't get out. "That's not the fucking point" we thought to ourselves as under privileged children from the Bronx. "Get that furry fucking thing out of here so we can sleep.....we have kindergarten tomorrow!" We have a long meeting and we need our rest. Then there was the foster home in the Bronx in an apartment in the Jackson public housing community (commonly referred to as the Projects). Our time at that foster home was also limited; only about a few months. At Jackson Projects, we were not the only children that were sharing the apartment with the foster parent.

Our foster mother had her own children, as well as another brother-sister pair. In total, there were seven children in this apartment that only had four rooms. Me and my sisters shared a room together while the other children were placed in the others. I don't remember much about this foster home except the feeling of not being very liked by the foster mother. This was the woman that if we as kids did something she didn't like or that would anger her, she would tell us "that's why you're not with your mother right now." Also, there was internal family bullying that was also felt by me and my sisters from the other "permanent" children, they would make us feel bad by telling us "that's why no one wants you to live with them." We understood this wasn't true and some of the other kids were just being mean for no reason. Also, Jackson

Projects were extremely close to where we grew up. Our family was literally within walking distance from where we slept. We knew we wouldn't be there for long and the judge would let us stay with our mother or our grandmother soon enough.

Once the decision was made by the Family Court to have us return to our family, we were ordered to live with our Grandmother (our mom's mother) until my mother was able to support us on her own. Which I'm here to tell you all reading this.....she never did. I love my mother very much and very much still talk to her as she has become sober from drug use, but we as her children have never been in her parental custody since 1988. Just as a reminder, I was born in 1983. But there is more to this portion of my life. Now, in 2020 as I write this memoir, I haven't learned to forgive my mother for never being there as a mother to us. There are feelings that I can't bury under the words of this memoir as a remedy for hurt. My mother is still not there, but frankly, I don't need her, and never did.

While living under the parental custody of my grandmother, we attempted to have as normal of a childhood as possible. The goal was to keep myself, my older sisters (and now my younger brother) under the custody of our grandmother for the duration of our lives until my mother was able to take care of us independently. My grandmother was and still is the backbone of our family. Her strong Christian faith and belief in the good of all people held our family together through the adversity of the 1980's into the early 1990's. My grandmother was the first role model for our family members to emulate ourselves after. She was a role model by being a medical professional; a practicing nurse. She also owned several homes in the Bronx (all within 7 city blocks of each other) for our family to live in so we were never homeless. All the homes she owned were occupied by my aunt's, our mother, uncles, and cousins of all ages.

My god as I write this, I can't believe how much she did for all of us. She was the blood of our family who would plan our family reunion every year, dress us for church every Sunday, take us to Hershey Park in Pennsylvania every year, and kept us safe from the dangerous influences of the streets. I love my grandmother because her love provided me with all the greatest memories of my life as a child. I smile when I think of the time I spent with my grandmother under her care. Eventually, my grandmother sought to allow my mother the opportunity to raise us as her own (with her still having legal custody of us). In an effort to build a strong family, my grandmother moved us back in with our mother, who was living in one of the homes my grandmother owned. We loved our mother dearly and couldn't wait to live with her again....that's what you're supposed to do.

Living with your mother is normal, and we desperately needed normal and stability during our chaotic childhood. Moving was easy as hell. My mother's house was a few avenues away on the same street. The house my grandmother owned was shared with many members of my family and was affectionately called "The Shack." The Shack was a two floor home with a one car garage, a balcony, basement, and backyard. This house sounds pretty nice from the outside looking in with words only, but it was a house that resembled the Freddy Kruger house in the "Nightmare on Elm Street" movie franchise. Our family was not rich, but at the same time we were very close to poverty (just above the line).

The Shack was always the spot for parties and activities in the neighborhood as my older sister (12 years older than me) would always throw parties for the other teenagers in the hood with food, DJs and Weed for everyone to smoke. When me and my other sisters were not being forced in our rooms to support my older sister's parties, we were entertaining ourselves with what was around us. In order to keep us in our rooms so that we didn't disturb her party, she would give us a red bucket with the word FIRE on it to use the bathroom in. Our sister loved us, but she was serious about her parties. We never used that shit bucket and took the risk of being spotted simply to use the bathroom with the toilet. There were no devices for us to use back then so our imagination was the only tool we had. But The Shack always had something for us to do. Whether it's playing hide and seek in an 8 room house, climbing to narrow hallway walls like Spiderman, or jumping in-out of the collapsed floor from the kitchen to the basement, we always had something to do when we were alone. We also knew where we could get a meal if we were ever hungry, which I felt like we always were.

At an early age, I learned to understand my surrounding resources and how to utilize them for our survival. Free lunch (at schools) during the summers was my favorite memory because school lunches and breakfast tasted a millions times better than what we were eating at our home (which sometimes was simply milk & cereal or a mayonnaise sandwich). We were given the unofficial responsibility of feeding ourselves in the absence of our mothers and fathers because that's the way things were. We were forced to grow up too fast, simply....because we could.

Once we moved in with our mother, it didn't take long for the supervision to start to fall off once again. We were once again mostly left on our own on multiple occasions with little information on when our mother would return. Time moves forward and I am now 8 - 9 years old and attending 4th Grade at P.S. 44. This was the age of the yellow shirt and blue pants/skirt uniform that all children wore to their classes in the beginning months of the school year to instill a standard of uniformity. There is nothing about that first year at P.S. 44 that I remember because....I wasn't there for the whole year. With no parents around most of the time to tell me to wash up or check my hygiene regularly, I manifested a condition on my right hand and I didn't know what it was called. My right hand became stiff and infected by some unknown pathogen and would cause large pustules (pus filled pimples) to form all over my hand. This also caused an odor and prohibited me from fully using my hand mechanically. It also caused a level of embarrassment because I never told my mother and thought it would go away eventually.

When the conditions persisted into the first week of school, I would go to school every day with my hand tucked into my sleeve, giving the appearance that I was missing my right hand. But I am Right-Handed and needed that hand to write in class. No problem, I would only expose my fingertips in order to write out my work. It didn't take long for the teacher to observe my bizarre writing technique and secretive handwriting nature. She approached me and told me to take my hand out of my shirt. "I don't want to," I replied. She approaches me and asks "are you ok William, what's wrong?" She takes my arm and slowly rolls my sleeve up exposing my diseased hand. She reacts shocked and takes me into the hallway to the administrative office.

I sat in the admin office for about thirty minutes while the school looked up the information for my other siblings who also went to the same school. To the teachers and staff, it looks like child neglect...and it was. Me and my other sisters (Charlene and Donna) are gathered in the administrative office where we are told we will be leaving with someone who will take care of us. We became scared collectively and started to cry together. We've been here before and we knew where we were going. A social worker approached us and walked us to an 18-PAX van where we were taken to a social services organization, and sent to a foster home in Central Islip NY. We never returned to our mother at the end of that school day, nor did we return to her care for the rest of our lives.

Reflection

Being able to successfully transition from one situation to the next is a skill that is practiced during our entire lives. Think back to your childhood and remember the situations you recall into your adult life often. Family stability or instability varies for everyone. The values placed upon you by your parents (or lack thereof) has made you into the adult you are today. Own your experiences for both the good and the bad. If you are not where you wish to be in life, look back at your childhood and recognize where it went right and where it went wrong. Success doesn't only happen when you are an adult, but it happens from your birth to your death. Being born was the first successful challenge you ever accomplished.

Meaning, you were born a success. It's that simple...You were born a success! You have the tools and the experiences to make yourself great at anything you choose. The best idea you can ever come up with is to never forget where you came from. Your story and the roots of your ambition will drive your success. Own the failures from your past experiences and celebrate your wins as much as possible. Even a small win must be celebrated, even if you're the only audience that knows what you've done. It took me a very long time to acknowledge some of my accomplishments and to be my own cheerleader. It took so long that for a while, I believed I was worthless. But looking back, I did great things that are unique to me and my experience. I am proud of myself. Be proud of who you are and never lose sight of your vision for greatness.

Transition Three:

From Low Threat to High Speed - <u>Send Me!</u>

The year is 2007 and I've been serving in the US Air Force for almost 5 years. The war in Afghanistan and Iraq (Global War on Terror) had been raging since 2003 and at this point, I had not been thrusted into the fires of combat as I desired. I left New York with one task in mind, to serve in a combat capacity in order to strike back at the ideological group or country that was responsible for so much death on American soil. Needless to say, I had been a Logistics Planner since 2003 which in my opinion, did nothing towards placing me in the action I seeked. It's not that I blindly wanted to get myself hurt or killed, but I wanted to protect others from getting hurt or killed by destroying the enemy, or giving my life in pursuit of glory. 2007 was filled with the growing frustration of being behind a desk while others went to war to fight. In describing my frustration to others, they are quick to ask me "well why did you go to the Air Force aka the Chair Force?"

Every service sees military combat in their own way and the Air Force was no different. From spotting that F-16 in the Bronx above my street, my fate was set; and so stayed my desire to fight and be a part of history through the dominance of Airpower. I knew there were opportunities for me to get

35

into the fight in the greatest Air Force in the world. Before I joined the Air Force as a Loadmaster, then as a Logistics Planner, I had dreams of becoming a member of Special Operations. Particularly, I wanted to join the Air Force as a Combat Controller (CCT). My recruiter (TSgt Ortiz) noticed my physical conditioning status when I was awaiting training in the Delayed Entry Program (DEP). He asked me in normal day to day conversation if I knew anything about Special Operations. I didn't even know that the Air Force had special ops, which the Air Force refers to this group as Special Tactics. I thought that capability only existed in the Navy and Army.

He gave me a small brochure which provided the basics of the role and responsibilities. I was hooked just on the information in the brochure alone. A Combat Controller's main mission is to secure Airfields and provide combat Air Traffic Control at the Assault Zone for follow-on forces. CCTs are the military descendants of the Army's Pathfinders in World War II. Pathfinders set up the initial drop zones for the Paratroopers of the 82nd and 101st airborne division during the Normandy Invasion on D-DAY. CCTs are the Air Force's top tier operators who most certainly would be involved with some of the most daring and historical missions during the Global War on Terror. I wanted.....no, I needed in. I trained as hard as I could...running, pushups, pull ups, strength training using the city as my gym and utilizing community fitness centers. In order for me to even have a shot at being accepted to training, I had to pass the Physical Abilities and Stamina Test (PAST). The PAST consisted of a 500 Meter swim, 8 Pull Ups, 53 Sit Ups, 58 Push Ups, and a 25 Meter underwater swim. All the events had to be completed in a particular order with strict times allowed for rest in between each event.

As fit as I was as a teenager, I was NOT ready for this test at all. In fact, it was the worst physical failure of my life at the time and a very funny story to tell others in the future. I swear my New York City confidence continued to show its ugly head at the wrong times which enabled me to assume I could accomplish anything. Why wouldn't I assume I could swim 500 Meters without practicing once.....I've been swimming at the beach and breaking into public pools since I was 7 years old. Swimming by myself was an activity I can do with ease. I got this....right?

Swimming was and is still NOT a subjective event. It takes practice skills and commitment to ensure efficiency in the water. You either can do it or you can't swim at all. So when it was time for me to take the PAST, the first event was swimming for the 500 meter requirement. I even went to the damn Speedo store and bought a tight ass speedo which I thought would reduce my drag in the water for MAXIMUM EFFICIENCY. Again, I had no practice or any technical training on the mechanics of proper swim techniques. Didn't matter, I was 18, hungry, and still mad as hell about September 11th. I strapped on my ridiculous looking/feeling speedo, got in the car with the recruiter, after a 2 hour drive to Fort Dix, New Jersey to use the pool, it's on! I was ready to prove myself ready for training and prepared to jump in the pool when told to do so. My recruiter was at the ready with the timer to count my laps and record my time for test compliance.

I stood at the edge of the pool ready to start. My heart was pounding as the whole event was 100% nerve racking. Here goes everything......Ready, Set, Go! I push off the wall and begin my swim with the worst fucking swim technique you can imagine. You know the technique, the one where your head is above water the whole time so you can see what's in front of you. Combined with the terrible form and my overall nervousness, I swam a total of 75 meters before I stopped from pure exhausting. Stopping during any portion of the PAST kills the entire test. I was done and failed my fist PAST. Even after that embarrassing failure, becoming a CCT member was always still a dream of mine and I absolutely looked up to those who performed that brave mission. 2007 was also a joyous year for me because my first child was born in the Bronx NY.

Jaden Gonzalez changed my life forever because now, I am not only responsible for my actions, but his as well. I thanked my girlfriend Katherine (who is now my loving wife) for giving me the gift of fatherhood. With my new family and my internal conflicts about my place in this world of war, I made the decision to change my Air Force job from a Logistics Planner, into anything that would get me into the war before it ended (which is ironic because as I write this, men and women are still fighting). I looked at the list of career options offered to me, knowing that I wanted to optimize my chances of choosing a career that will provide me the opportunity to fight or directly support the war effort. I chose careers from the Critical Shortage list as they were undermanned and needed to be filled with bodies as soon as possible. Out of the critical shortage list, I ensured I selected jobs that would send me directly to combat by conducting some research beforehand.

I narrowed my selection to three Air Force careers, Flight Engineer, Aerial Gunner, and Special Investigations. Since my physical standards were not ready to take and pass a PAST, I did not choose any special ops careers such as Pararescue, Combat Control, Special Ops Weather, or Tactical Air Control (TACP). Flight Engineers and Aerial Gunners both would have placed me on combat aircraft such as the AC-130, the HH-60, MH-53, or the MC-130. Special Investigations on the other hand was always another career I wanted based on my childhood aspirations of being in Law Enforcement. The selection process for Special Investigations (aka OSI) was a little different than the normal Air Force Specialty Code (AFSC) change process. Simply put, I chose the Aerial Gunner career field because it offered the best chance for me to see combat as all the aircraft that Aerial Gunners operated were combat aircraft (AC-130, HH-60, MH-53). Selecting the Flight Engineer career field may have placed me on Combat Support aircraft such as the C-5, C-130, E-3 or E-4 aircraft which were never a viable option for me. Excited towards my future prospects, I submitted my package as soon as I was able to and got an approval for Aerial Gunner training which started in 1 year. I was so happy and saw the amazing people, places, and missions I will experience flash before my eyes and enter my dreams as I slept. But with the new approval comes more changes for me and my new family. I would be starting a new transition from one career to another, I will go from a support role to the supported role, and lastly I will train for combat rather than sending others to it in my stead. Changes were coming again, and me and my new family were headed straight for it.

I re-enlisted for another 6 years in the US Air Force to support my new family and my new career as an Aerial Gunner. This career choice was a no brainer for me because I have always been fascinated with the bravery it took for those men and women to fight during World War II during the air campaign over Europe. My highest admiration went to the aircrews of the B-17 Flying Fortress (Bomber Aircraft) that were flown over occupied Europe. This 4-engine aircraft had ten crew positions: Pilot, Co-Pilot, Navigator, Bombardier, Flight Engineer, Radio Operator, and four Aerial Gunners. Being "Enlisted" in the military is considered the tougher part of military service because the Enlisted men and women executed the tasks and orders of the Officers. We are called the backbone of the military because without the Enlisted force, the military would not be able to support itself to stand up and fight. For the crews of the B-17 and their respective positions, it was true that the Officers did the flying, but the enlisted did the fighting in the air. Knowing that every mission you launched may either be an easy (milk) run, or the hardest fight you'll ever experience took balls and guts not seen ever before in history. I looked up to the legacy of Aerial Gunners and was proud and satisfied with my career choice, for I would become a rich part of history that made a difference on the battlefield to win our nation's wars. While I prepared to begin my training which was less than 60 days away, we (the Gonzalez family) must move out of our house on Andrews Air Force base in Maryland. Me and my wife....well mostly me, packed our things in storage and her and our son head back to New York City to stay with our family while I complete training. Training to be an Aerial Gunner took several courses within its "pipeline."

The first course was Aircrew fundamentals......yup I'm back in fundamentals again! This time I have no desire to quit as I have chosen a combat oriented career in the air with a rich history of victory. The next course after successful completion of fundamentals was the Aerial Gunner Apprentice course. This course teaches the students about Aerial Gunner history, aircraft introduction, basic aircraft systems, weapon system operations, defensive systems, & emergency procedures associated with the MH-53, HH-60, and AC-130 weapon systems. I almost didn't graduate the apprentice course because I had failed the final exam the day before graduation. Up until that point, I had no problem passing my exams with the 85% required (per the aircrew standard). I became so nervous during the final exam because I had placed an enormous amount of pressure on myself not to fail. If I don't pass I won't be awarded my Aircrew Wings and I'll have to go back to logistics....I would've failed myself...I won't see any combat and fight for my country....I'll disappoint my new son....It all rides on me passing this last exam.

Of course I failed the final and had to retake a test. This sucked because I missed the opportunity to walk on stage and receive my Aircrew Wings with the rest of our class. My first taste of humble pie was gross and I never wanted another piece of ratchet metaphorical food. I took the night to review all my class material again and truly committed everything not only to memory, but to an internal level of understanding leading to comprehension. I took the test the next day and passed with flying colors and confidence. Now that I have been awarded my aircrew wings....I can start flying and call myself a Gunner.......Hell No, not yet. There are still 5 more levels of training within the pipeline before I can become a Mission Qualified Aerial Gunner that is able to perform all tasks as a competent crew member.

The next course was the water survival course which teaches students how to survive if you crash into the ocean with limited supplies. This was an extremely fun and rewarding course because my weaknesses in the pool were on full display once again. I still didn't know how to even tread water, which made treading for 60 seconds feel like an eternity. I still couldn't swim underwater well and we had to swim 15 meters. I was instructed to use the remedial underwater rope to pull myself across, and my swim technique was still shit...but I managed to swim 25 meters without dying. Compared to my skill level 7 years ago, there is not much improvement.

The only good thing about that portion was I didn't have to wear the "I can't swim" helmet that was colored yellow while everyone else's was black. Water survival school was only two days and ended with an indoor ocean ditching exercise that was extremely realistic. Inside the Olympic size pool, the instructors would turn off the lights, simulate large waves, heavy rain (medium pressure fire hose in your face) thunderstorms, and high winds using large turbo fans. The next day of training the underwater egress trainer, which simulated how to escape a sinking helicopter. In the same Olympic pool, there is a fake helicopter fuselage that is lowered into the 15 ft deep water than rolled upside down. We completed five dunks with the last dunk being blindfolded (to simulated night-time conditions). I wished the dunker trainer was the first water class that we had because it builds the student's water confidence a lot faster than the others. There is a daunting feeling knowing you are strapped into a seat in this big fake helicopter, water rushing up from the floor to your face; all while you're flipped upside down in the sinking apparatus. It is very uncomfortable, but the training is invaluable in case you ever have to use it during an actual crash landing. The next course on the menu was Combat Survival training.

This was the first mind-fuck during the pipeline I experienced where I didn't know how far training would be pushed. Combat Survival is a course that continues with no breaks or weekends off. The course length can vary depending on student performance and the completing of objectives. This was one of my favorite courses because it was beautiful to do all of the camping activities in the woods of Washington State that I've never been able to do growing up in the Bronx.

Hiking, mountain climbing, mountain falling, and aspects of hunting such as skinning and cooking captured animals was a total new experience for me. The fun parts of Combat Survival school like navigating through the woods and sleeping in your own build-from-scratch shelter was reminiscent of television shows such as Alone or Survivor. The not-so fun portions of Survival School were the different and stressful experiences which prepared the aircrews for the harsh reality captured and imprisonment by a not so friendly enemy who sought to extract information, torture, or kill us. The training was very effective and realistic, I have never forgotten those hard lessons learned during that hot summer. Let's just say I can still feel the pain I experienced there from the mountainous terrain and the instructors who were allowed to strike us. Survival School was the first time I felt like I was truly training for war and my hopes of getting into the fight would be assured so long as I survived the course. By now it was 2008 and some of the greatest battles of the Afghanistan and Iraq theater had already occurred. When was I going to get some of this history that I read about and strive to be a part of? Once I graduated Combat Survival School, I headed out to Kirtland Air Force Base in New Mexico to begin the flying portion of my training. The first portion of flying training is all academic followed by rides in the simulator.

The academic portion was the most challenging portion of my training because the expectation given to students is that you teach yourself. Sure there are instructors, but the feeling I constantly felt was that no one is there to instruct you, the instructors were there to observe if you can do the job. The feeling I felt was instructors wanted to see which student wanted it the most by putting in the work to teach themselves. Yes we had classes that taught us about helicopter dynamics and aircraft systems, but there was very little time for in-depth discussion concerning system operations as the course had a strict schedule to follow. Additionally, the instructors were assigned to different blocks of training at the same time and would have their schedule change daily. I learned a ton about true flexibility at this course because you would have to call the school every day to see what portion of training you were going to receive (in no linear order). One day you would learn about defensive systems and countermeasures, the next you would learn about aircrew resource management. But before you even start class, you must receive your training materials such as regulations, checklist, technical orders, and standard operating procedures. The aircraft technical order (referred to as the Dash-1) was over 1000 pages of reading about systems operations, emergency procedures, power & cruise data charts, and operational checklist items. There was no room for bull-shit during this course and since I've always considered myself academically challenged, I studied my ass off every day of the week during the first phase of training to ensure I didn't fall behind. Once the academic portion completed with successful completion of our block tests, we moved on to simulator training.

As an Aerial Gunner, the only simulator we had to take before actual flying was the Gunnery simulator (which placed the student in a virtual helicopter using headsets and gun emplacements). This was the equivalent of shooting a machine gun game at the Arcade with a virtual reality headset with a 190 degree view. While this was exactly like playing a video game with the seriousness of combat incoming/outgoing fire, it would make you sick to your stomach due to the virtual environment creating a vertigo effect. Throwing up was common as the rocking motion, low light, and reduced field of view would make hell for your sense of balance. I couldn't be happier to complete the simulator because it sucked, but also, it taught us that we were not just there to shoot em up bang bang. We had to scan, communicate, and think of the importance of the missions we will participate in. While the instructor would shoot at us within the virtual environment, we would naturally get fixated on the threat and forget about what the rest of the aircraft and crew were doing.

During another training iteration, he would drift the aircraft into a tree or cause the helicopter to overshoot the landing zone (missing our objective). This was the lesson, to pay the fuck attention to what's happening around you and stay ahead of the aircraft (a term that was beat into our heads throughout training). Having never fired a machine gun up to this point in my life, the "War Wagon" was by far the coolest portion of ground academic training. The instructors rigged an electronically actuated and operated machine gun called the GAU-2 (Minigun) to the back of a box trailer which could be towed with an F-150 truck or equivalent. We would pack up some ammo, a small lunch, and head out to the range located deep within the base (which was a mountain range in the middle of nowhere).

Applying everything we learned in the classroom about weapon operations, emergencies, crew resource management, communicating, & safety, we took aim down the weapon, flipped the power switch on and fired. THE BEST FEELING EVER was firing this 6-barreled machine gun which spun so fast it fired at a rate of 2000 & 4000 rounds a minute by pressing a low rate or high rate button. Things became more real for us as this weapon would be used to kill someone at a rate of 33 rounds per second. Imagine being hit with that much firepower for every second of your soon to be short ass life. This was a deadly weapon that struck fear into the enemy by the volume of firepower and the sheer noise it made once fired. It sounded like a dragon belching fire down your neck and it won't stop until you are dead and completely unrecognizable to your loved ones.

Keep in mind, I still haven't set foot into an aircraft to place all the ground training to appropriate use. But the time is fast approaching when ground training comes to an end and we take our final ground evaluation. I am proud to say, I passed my final ground evaluation and headed to the flightline to await training in my military aircraft of choice....the HH-60G Pavehawk helicopter. If the ground instructors were the experienced old school civilian aviators that had no more fucks to give, the flightline instructors were true assholes who had plenty of fucks to give. Sharing was caring, and these flightline instructors were some of the most experienced Pavehawk crews the Air Force had to offer. Their missions were legendary and spanned from the participation in the recovery of Marcus Latrell (Lone Navy Seal Survivor), to supporting special operation insertions during the initial invasion of Iraq in 2003. These were true American heros to look up to and I looked forward to their instruction. Of course, these old school crusty Non-Commissioned Officers were not interested in simply imparting their knowledge on every person who walked through the schoolhouse doors. You had to earn their respect and their knowledge through practical performance. It was a game of trust...mainly, can you be fucking trusted to do your fucking job in combat. Some of the best training I ever experienced was while an instructor was yelling "what the fuck are you doing Gunner....where the fuck is two" (the other aircraft)?

The day arrives when it is my turn to fly in my crew position with an angry ass Gunner instructor who wanted to make sure I didn't fall out the fucking helicopter. We performed our pre-flight inspection on the inside and outside the helicopter with the instructor asking you questions about "what is this...what is the warning about this component...what else could you be doing right now?" After not receiving a "no step" for not fucking up my presented knowledge of the aircraft, we await for the pilots to arrive and start the aircraft by running the Before Starting Engines & Starting Engines checklist. The engine is started, all calls are made to the ground controller, and the rotors are spinning at 100 percent. The noise emitting from the aircraft is so loud that I barely hear the crew talking to each other. The checklist is complete and we're ready for taxi down the taxiway. The pilot says "Coming Forward"...we reply "Clear Forward Right".....Clear Forward Left." We move....no more than 15 knots on the taxiway to find the takeoff runway that will guide us when we leave the base. During the taxi from the parking spot to the runway, there is constant chatter on the radios between the aircraft, air traffic control, crew members and instructors. It's never just quiet while operating a military aircraft on a busy military runway shared with the civilian airport. There is always someone talking over the intercom system and activity going on inside and outside the aircraft so attention to detail is paramount. We received clearance to take off and my heart started racing from the rush of adrenaline coursing through my body.

The aircraft lifts off and we begin our training flight with the rush and smell of air mixed with aircraft JP8 fuel. What a magnificent feeling it was to fly above the earth and stare down at the landmarks becoming smaller and smaller. All this is happening while I am wildly afraid of heights, but being in the aircraft as an active crewmember is different. You have a level of control unlike simply standing atop a tall building where the fear stems from slipping or being pushed by the wind to your smashed death. Crewmembers are secured with safety belts (called a Gunner's Belt) and seat belts. Collectively we control how high we ascend, descend, and how fast we travel through the air based on crew resource management and aircraft power available. The level of control we maintain is very comforting. Also, the realization that if you were to fall out of the sky because of a malfunction, you can take peace that your death may be quick and painless. Flight after flight, I become more competent & comfortable in my abilities to function as an active crewmember and not just as a passenger enjoying the ride. If you were not doing something in the aircraft to either keep in operating at efficient levels or keeping the other crew safe, you were behind and that could get you and your crew killed. We practiced landings, take-offs, insertion & extraction of special ops teams, air refueling, aerial gunnery, emergency procedures, & defensive maneuvers. After about 80 hours of flying, it's time for the student to experience their first mission evaluation (check-ride). This is an exercise that tests everything you've learned from the beginning of the course to end; at night under night vision goggles. The mission profile is the rescue of a down fighter pilot in a contested area with a known & verified enemy presence.

This was my last mission flight check-ride before I graduated from the schoolhouse. The evaluation started normal until we approached the Alternate Insertion Extraction (AIE) portion of the flight. As the Gunner, I was responsible for preparing the AIE devices for the simulated team's entry and exit out the aircraft. After I completed pulling in and securing the Rope Ladder (a device used by teams to climb into the helicopter from water or a minefield), we took-off in order to enter the pattern for the next iteration task. This is where in the mission profile I fucked up. The next event was preparing the rappel rope for use and deployment outside the aircraft. While we were still climbing during the take-off, I began trying to stay ahead of the aircraft by readying my rappel rope...heads down, in the climb. Hugh fucking mistake (I'll explain why shortly). My evaluator saw my mistake and didn't say a word. The flight continued for another 2 hours until we completed all tasks and returned to base. We landed and placed all of our gear away with myself feeling good about my performance.

This was my last flight before going operational and heading out to Okinawa Japan. We arrived at the debrief as a crew and talked about the flight and the training objectives that we met and ones we did not. Still riding on cloud nine because, in my mind, I had a great flight. Probably the best fight I've had since arriving to flight training. I met with my evaluator privately after the crew briefing. He states without hesitation "I have to Hook you" as soon as we sit. Hooking is slang for failure in the flying community. I didn't take the news very well and asked what I did wrong. I failed the entire evaluation because my head was down manipulating the rappel rope during a critical phase of flight...take-off. Being young and stupid I didn't take the news well and signed my which told the world I failed.

Just like all training in the military, I get one more shot to pass or I will be removed out of the program. Another helpful critique my evaluator gave me was my level of assertiveness in the aircraft was lacking. Specifically, when it comes to communicating with my simulated teams in the back of the cabin. My evaluator told me at the beginning of the flight that he would pretend to be the PJ, SEAL, CCT team leader. He wanted to evaluate how I communicated with the team leader during flight phases and under stress. "You have to move the team out the way if they prohibit you from preparing your equipment" he informed me. It doesn't matter if you're working with the most high speed team in the world....this is your aircraft." Be more assertive" when needed. My evaluator, acting as a team member, refused to move out my way to test what I would do in that situation.

I'm glad I failed that flight because he provided valuable lessons to me that I would use during my continuation training and in the combat zone. My next opportunity to fly and re-check to graduate came the following week. Remembering the lessons from my first and only Hook ride, I successfully passed my re-check and graduated Aerial Gunner Initial Qualification Training. I also had the chance to practice my assertiveness in the aircraft when my evaluator (another instructor who was told about my lack of assertiveness with the team). To test me, my instructor became a fucking bump in my way and didn't move out my way when told to do so. Keep in mind, my evaluator was an experienced Senior Master Sergeant with over 2500 flight hours and god knows how many combat hours. He was in my way, blocking me from prepping my Fast Rope for the next event. I screamed at him to get the fuck out the way and proceeded to physical shoved him to the center of the aircraft. I later apologized for shoving him....but he replied "sometimes that's what you need to do for new inexperienced team guys." He told me to stay in the books and never lose your edge simply because you've graduated.

8 months later after starting my journey into my new career, I was an initial qualified aircrew member for the HH-60G helicopter. I was on my way to my first duty station to receive even more advanced Aerial Gunnery, Water operations (day

and night), Shipboard operations, & Combat Search and Rescue Task Force training. Being a graduate of an Air Force's aviation courses was one of the proudest moments of my life, second only to the birth of my children. Deep down inside, I've always wanted my children to look back at my service and be proud of my accomplishments. I wanted to provide my children with an example for them to always strive to exceed expectations...to never let the world tell them what they can or can't do...to be the very best they can be.

There are no limitations that were placed upon myself when it came to my professional goals. My son still has a picture of me and him in my flight suit as I attended training to become a Combat Search and Rescue Aerial Gunner. It makes me proud to be a positive example for him to emulate in his future. I returned to Andrews AFB to see my family again and to pack our things to ship off to Okinawa Japan. My now wife Katherine and our son Jaden begin our trip across the pond to Okinawa. This is our first trip out of the country as a family and we have a lot to learn about how to still take care of ourselves in this new world of military service. Although I have been with my wife for 7 years at this point (2009), this is our first major event as a newly married couple.

The trip to Japan was just as exciting because we also visited Seattle Washington for the first time and did touristy things such as visit the space needle. There was nothing I enjoyed more than falling asleep and waking up in the same bed as my Wife and our 2 year old Son on our way to the unknown. We boarded the plane and embarked on our 13 hour flight from the US to Okinawa with the feeling of butterflies being in our stomach from the anticipation. What will it be like, who will we meet, what will we eat, what will the beaches be like? After a grueling flight which made us hate planes for the next year, we arrived on the island of Okinawa. As soon as we exited the plane onto the tarmac at Kadena Air Base, the humidity of the pacific island smacks you and your momma in the face with an overt feeling of "holy hell it's hot here!"

It's if the heat was manifested into a giant hand that slapped you on your face and squeezed your cheeks together like your grandparents who haven't seen you in forever. We met our sponsors (E-Pott, T-Pott & J. Schramm) who gave us a ride to our room and gave us a brief tour of the base and the surrounding areas. We were given about 2 days to get settled before I showed up for work. On my first day, I felt the weight of the responsibilities placed upon me as these men and women will one day depend on me to protect them and save others. I walked into the building that was filled with heroes from the war in Afghanistan and Iraq.

Heroes who lived up to the motto "These things we do, that others may live." Heroes who responded to natural events such as hurricane Katrina and will respond to the Tohoku Earthquake and Tsunami on mainland Japan in the future. I loved these men and women from the very first moment I stepped into the building and ensured that I gave them 100% of my effort to learn my job to the best of my ability. And maybe, give my life so that others can have the chance to live on. Training was over...now it was time to start operating.

Charlie Transition

Consider your future choices as opportunities to learn from mistakes that have not been attempted. Every lesson that will be learned from the choices you make will reinforce your personal & professional growth into a better individual. Do not shy away from the hard choices you will make and always consider the effects your choices will have on your family. Do not doubt yourself! Don't let fear of the unknown dictate what choices to make and which ones to never make. Look fear and doubt in the face and realize you are in control over everything that happens to you (even the bad things that will occur). Do not blame others for your choices. Choices are not mistakes. Mistakes are only lessons if you choose to learn from them. Make more mistakes in your life by trying new things and not being afraid to fail.

Failure is essential for healthy growth and intellectual maturity. No scientist got it right on the first try. In fact, the best minds of our society, scientifically speaking, have a whole list of failures that they can share with the world if you search for them. Transitioning careers is a hard and scary choice because it forces you to learn new skills, new tactics, meet new people, and create new habits. With all those new experiences will create a newer emotionally intelligent entity within yourself that is capable of adapting to endless change. The will to transition effectively comes from your adaptability to change. That adaptability is only nurtured through learning new things by choice. Make your own damn choices and commit to the tough lessons that will be learned by embracing your inevitable failures. Own it! Commit to learning something new and practice your ability to adapt rapidly to external and internal changes.

Transition Four:

From self-preservation to acceptance - <u>Prepared to go!</u>

Choosing the military as my career for the past eight years up to this point in my life, I never felt the burden of what true military service was about until I joined the Air Force's elite Combat Search and Rescue squadrons (CSAR). Unknown to many (especially those who were never in the military) these units were responsible for some of the most daring rescues under fire during the Vietnam war, The Gulf war, and during the Global War on Terror (Iraq & Afghanistan).

CSAR units are referred to by the military as the Pedros or Jollys. When military operations commence where our brave men & women have to take the fight to the enemy, the military Commander will not start the mission without CSAR support. Rescue squadrons are the premier search and rescue force tasked (at all cost) with traveling behind enemy lines under fire from small arms, surface to air missiles, or other aircraft to rescue downed Aircrews for the entire Department of Defense. We possess the aircraft, weapons, tactics, and Pararescue specialist to perform this mission better than any other unit in the world. To sum this up, CSAR is the military's

911, because even Navy Seals need to call for help. Aside from the tactics we employ as a formation of two helicopters and a combined crew of 14, flying under combat conditions is inherently dangerous work within any profession. Every day I reported to work, the potential for dying because of an aircraft fire, explosion, collision were high. There was no flight that was easier than the less if your goal was to be the best. Flying is loud, cold, hot, uncomfortable, and at times terrifying. But fear can be combated and silenced through the application of knowledge. Fear is manifested within oneself because of the unknown. When we don't know how events will occur or how they will end, we can become fearful from our natural survival instincts which forces the preservation of life.

When military knowledge is increased because of drills, exercises, and advanced continuation training, the fear is slowly diminished or eliminated in total. We learned to control our fear in the aircraft, take more risk, and build tougher skin as was expected of our profession. Our profession (within the profession of arms) was flying into armed conflict to rescue someone else's son, sister, mother or father...That Others May Live. Being afraid of the helicopter malfunctions like the engines shutting off, causing us to fall out the sky from 1000 feet can be terrifying....but only if you knew nothing about helicopter aerodynamics. All you could imagine was the aircraft falling out the sky in a tumble and hitting the ground with such force that it caused a large explosion...killing everyone onboard.

Now, think of that same scenario with increased operational knowledge. We practiced this scenario every month. We would pretend that our engines were malfunctioning causing us to fall. We would perform an Autorotation to the ground initiated at or above 500 feet above the ground. An Autorotation is similar to a flower that is dropped from high. It spins and descends controlled to the ground. In a helicopter, the rotors will still continue to spin without power input because of the upwind of air during the fall. Basic hydraulic function allows the rotor's pitch to be controlled causing an increased or decreased spin. The fall becomes controlled all the way to the ground with the potential of survival so long as the rotors are left parallel to the ground (causing lift or weight as needed). Conduct this maneuver enough times and your fear will become significantly reduced to the prospect of crashing.

But fear was never completely eroded from the minds of military personnel. Fear caused us to critically think, analyze threats, and fight harder for one another in the heat of battle. One of my fears was the fear of letting my crew down when the metal met the meat. I feared letting my crew and fellow squadron mates down and tried to prove every day that I will fight hard to do my job, protect them and kill everyone who tried to stop me. Killing…..a concept that we all talk about but never experienced until we are thrown into the shit. As an Aerial Gunner, my job was to ensure defensive systems on the aircraft were operational at all times. I learned everything I could about how our weapons (GAU-2 and GAU-18) operated down to the smallest component to the largest bullet. This was my job and I was proud to be the reason I was either saving life, or taking it to save the lives of others. But fear of being killed or the killing of others was always present in the beginning of my career.

I committed to increasing my knowledge about the weapon system, my knowledge about the enemy, my knowledge about our tactics, and my knowledge of the Law of Armed Conflict. When we flew Aerial Gunnery sorties where we would practice terminal operations and defensive tactics against stationary targets, the more we flew, the more comfortable we were in the air. The more we shot on the range, the more we can operate safely behind the weapon. The more targets we hit, the more confident we will be killing. Make no mistake, we were practicing the art of killing people, destroying equipment or vehicles. You will hope your bullets destroy the selected target, because that's what they will become....targets.

People are targets, the enemy are targets, and the terrorists who will try to kill you are targets. I learned not to care about their lives or their purpose. They shot at me, they are a target and will be destroyed as such. My fear of killing is greatly reduced within the short span of one year. I have become an effective crew member and weapon operator for my CSAR crew. To become an effective military operator, the reality that death may come for you at any time must be accepted. Even during training, we must be ready to die and be ok with it. I carried this way of thinking with myself during my time as a combat crew member because it enabled me to focus. Focus on my task, and suppress my fears of the unknown. Acceptance of death is mentally freeing. But not all my colleagues shared my philosophy. There was still hope that lingered in the hearts of some of the older enlisted members who had 5 - 8 combat deployments under their belt. I felt their fear when I would fly with them. They've been there and done that with many hours of flying and combat missions under their belt. I respected these members of our unit but at the same time, felt they did not respect me because I was new, young, and I acted without fear.

This is not to say I acted reckless or unsafe in the aircraft. This was never the case...I just learned to accept death as a daily part of my job. This was felt and received by my senior crew members and caused contention between me and them. Contention to the point where one of my senior crew members would tell me. "I have so much to worry about, I can't worry about you when we fly". Who the fuck says that? We fly, fight, and die together. I was always prepared to do everything for my crew additional to my own duties in the aircraft. To hear that from my senior members who were also my instructors...that they didn't have my back during peacetime operations, would they have my back when the bullets started flying? To me, this did not matter because I didn't give in to the fear of letting my teammates down, no matter what our disagreements were. I would protect them. Even if they wouldn't do the same for me.

My responsibility is to eliminate or reduce my fear of underperforming and to protect others, I must be able to call myself out on my weakness and bullshit whenever it presents. Weaknesses will grow if they are not checked or strengthened through deliberate action. As mentioned earlier, my weakness was still my ability to swim. How will I save myself or others if we crash our helicopter in the water? Fear is a cancer and will grow internally if it is not dealt with swiftly.

One of the missions for Combat Search and Rescue is to rescue crew members in an ocean environment. Remember, this is combat rescue so we train for the most difficult water rescues performed in contested radar environments, at night using Night Vision Goggles (NVGs) with the threat of enemy surface naval forces or submarines attacking our operations. We would fly to the last known point of the person that needs to be rescued and conduct a search of the area if needed. If it's daytime, the search is relatively painless. But when its dark.....It's fucking dark! With 0 - 10% moon luminosity, the horizon that discerns between the sky and the water is difficult to detect with the naked eye. Imagine hovering above the open ocean with your eyes closed and descending. How much would your insides clinch until you yell stop? Lucky for us, our helicopters have the best avionics suite and can inform us when we are as low as 5 feet in the dark of night. We would locate the survivor and insert our Pararescueman in the water. We approach the water to a level of ten feet from the water surface and drop the PJs in the water. So in about 5 minutes from finding our survivor, we maneuvered our 22,000 lbs. helicopter and hovered 10 feet above the water....at night with NVGs on. Fuck YES I needed to learn how to swim! For the love of god I needed this skill! How did I get this far into my career with no swim capability...hovering 10 feet above the ocean in a floating truck? Luckily, my good friend Walter took me under his tutelage and taught my city ass how to swim in the water by improving my technique & efficiency. While we lived in Okinawa Japan, there was a Marine base named Foster that had a 25 meter pool that was heated and open for swimming at night. After a few lessons with my great friend, I was able to tread and swim enough to be dangerous in the water.

To his credit, my pal Walter taught me way more during my military career other than just swimming. He taught me how to relax, look at the bigger picture, and not rush to complete all my tasks in the next five minutes. I professionally expected myself to place 20 lbs. of shit in a 10 lb. bag. Walter saw my moves and would gently tell me "nah, you don't need to do that now." Besides him being a year older than me, Walter had lived a whole life of his own that is worth reading if he ever gets the chance to write about it. This man had been flying in the Air Forces for almost 5 years at this point and had many hours both in the MH-53 Pavelow (Special Operations medium lift helicopter) and the HH-60G (Pavehawk). Beside his life experiences, he was a fanatics Flight Engineer who helped me understand the components of the helicopter whenever I was struggling to grasp the concept of systems operations. Also, he used to be a lifeguard, so having him as my instructor was beneficial from every angle. Combined with my Underwater Egress Training, my ability to survive in an over-water crash was increased.

My knowledge increased for swimming and for helicopter Night Water operations which reduced my fear in the water at night. I could perform my combat mission with more efficiency and lethality simply from increasing my knowledge. Now, I thought I was ready for my first combat deployment and begged my superiors to send me with the next group going to Afghanistan. It was all I wanted, to help the fight to be there for my country as so many others have in the past before me.

This concept of defending oneself and others is not a natural trait. The will to fight is not born within all people, it is cultural. Warriors are bred from the fires of conflict between one or more entities. Although America has a vast history of combat (compared to its young age), the culture of our society is mostly peaceful. We are not born into the world and taught about the violence of action against an opposing enemy. We believe in peace and strive to find peace in every moment in our lives. But growing up in New York City, I have experienced violence against me and have witnessed it against others. These events were not meant to happen to us because we are not a warrior nation. There are very few warriors within our nation who are later trained to fight our nation's wars, but this is largely due to repetition, the necessity of protecting because of provocation, and a capitalist need for income.

When I returned to live with my father after spending four years in a foster home in Long Island NY, I had to learn who my father really was. After all, my dad was only around for limited amounts of time within my life and never deliberately cared for me until I became 10 years old. I never knew why this was....maybe he didn't make enough money to support me, maybe he wasn't ready to be a full-time dad, maybe my mother didn't let him. I remembered my father visiting us and taking us for a treat every once in a while throughout my childhood, but I lived mostly with my Grandmother and mother until my father filed for custody of me.

This was a hard period because my other three siblings were still in the foster home and did not leave with me because we each had different fathers. Saying goodbye to my siblings was hard to do knowing how much I loved them. Now living with my father, I started a new transition where I had to adapt to his rules, ways, methods, and habits. My father was a hard worker and had provided a good life for himself as a single man who had children. My father was never married and had another son (my older half-brother) who lived in California at the time. My father was a United States Marine from 1952-1955.

He did not serve during the Korean War, but spent his service in Okinawa as a postal clerk, mostly drinking and partying from what I gathered from his stories. My will to serve did not come from my father, nor did my spirit to fight. The lessons I learned from my father were to always ask questions and to defend myself. My father's nick-name was Joker because he was the life of the party, a ladies man, and told the best jokes to make everyone around him laugh. Joker was also a heavy drinker who had internal anger against the world that he would take out on me.

I learned this hard truth as a 10 year-old when my father punched me in the face for answering a question the wrong way, not to his liking when he was on a Budweiser binge. I never slept much on the nights he would drink because he would always force me to wake up and talk to him. Mostly about bullshit with the confusing context of "I love you son" thrown in as if that made the abuse acceptable. My dad would talk my ear off knowing that I had school the next morning. 1 AM......he would wake me to talk to him because he was down about something. I would talk to him because....he's my dad. He would also have these stupid drills in the middle of the night testing my speed to get to him from the living room (where I slept in his one bedroom apartment).

He would scream "William come quick" so I would hurry thinking my father was in trouble....and its him fucking with me, drunk off his ass. And when I wouldn't get there fast enough, he would hit me and tell me to try again. I did, crying the entire time trying to get my response time faster. My father would beat me with his hands and with his belt always when he was drunk off beer and depressed about something that happened to him that day or in his life. When I returned home from school one day and I saw my dad was in the kitchen with the overhead light on, I knew I had to expect not to sleep much and plan either my escape or defense.

Sometimes, I would hide in my father's closet all night to avoid him. Not making a sound as he looks for me, then calls the police as he assumes I am missing. Meanwhile, I'm in his closet sleeping, waiting for the noise to stop followed by my father's drunk snoring. This couldn't last forever, but how long was I supposed to endure this. When I turned 14, my dad once again woke me up in the middle of the night to bother me while drunk. It's always the same course of action....he wakes me, we talk, I answer his questions, I ask to go back to sleep, he hits me hard.

Knowing this I knew when the escalation to violence would occur. When he would hit me again (always in my face), I stood up this time and screamed "leave me alone"...Swinging my fist to the temple of his head as hard as I could....connected...and down he went. I had knocked out my drunk father who had abused me physically for the last 3 years. My father was 63 years old. I was never proud of this moment. I got dressed as fast as I could and ran out of the apartment stepping over my father's motionless body. I ran down 7 flights of stairs crying as hard as I could. I was hurt...I just hurt my dad....was this my life?

I walked to my older sister's house and spent a few hours with her, just long enough to sleep because I had school in a few hours. I learned to have a fighting spirit, but not in the method you would assume or for the best reasons. I had to defend myself, even if that meant hurting others to do so. Hurting my father was a low moment of my teenage years, but it taught me the value of patience and acting only when the response is Just. Violence against one another should always be the last resort in a functioning society.

9/11 was the most just cause I've ever witnessed...to fight back and defend was and always will be the right thing to do. Itching and ready to prove to myself and others that I can and will keep them safe, my Flight Chief, who was my leader at the time, tells me "you are not ready." What? How so? I feel ready, I've completed all the training & flight requirements. Why am I not allowed to go on this deployment? "You need more time in the aircraft and you just got here with your family." This was hard to hear because that was the point of joining the military was to Fly, Fight, and Win. It took me some time to understand what he was trying to relay to me. Clearly to him, I needed more time flying and understanding of the crews I flew with. At this point I accumulated almost 150 hours of flying (which included my time at the school house). I sat the first deployment out but the next one was not far behind as it was only 8 months away. This was too long to the young 26 year old who just wanted to be sent to combat before the war ended. In between deployments, we flew, shot guns, attended courses, learned new tactics, and trained with other forces on Okinawa like the Japanese military, Marine Force Recon, and Army Special Forces (1st Special Forces Group). 8 months passed, spin up training is completed, auxiliary training has been accomplished, comfort level is 1000. Send Me!

The period before boarding the plane heading towards a war zone is a somber moment and provides time for you to reflect with your other teammates, yourself, and your family. The bureaucracy of military logistics is based on timelines and deadlines. Certain events must be accomplished at H-Hour or on D-DAY based on the hurry up and wait method. But once all the last minute checks are completed and the forms for your records are reviewed another hundred times, it's time to say goodbye to your friends and family. Because of the length of this current conflict, our military members have become desensitized to the act of deploying. This can be great, but can also turn around and become a terrible attribute of current military service. Before, wars were fought till the end and the men and women were entrusted to get the job done or die trying, the expectation of survival was limited. This allowed the men and women to focus on the deadly task of warfighting while eliminating the distraction of hope. Even though this was my first deployment, this was one of my crew mate's 8th. He has gone to war and come back eight times.

This lucky streak can provide a false sense of hope for those charged with fighting the war..."this is just another deployment" I'll be back shortly. Everyone thinks like this, and everyone also becomes surprised when members do not come home because their helicopter has crashed...killing everyone on board. I made it a point within myself to not expect to come back. Not that I didn't want to, I loved my family and my lovely wife and awesome children to the fullest extent possible. I am more fearful of dying in combat because I didn't give the enemy the respect they deserve by committing my life, blood, sweat, tears, and focus solely on saving lives and killing every enemy combatant who wants to kill me with extreme prejudice.

I boarded that C-17 with my helicopter crew members with a focus towards accomplishing my goals with zero distraction. We arrived in Afghanistan under the cover of night to avoid incoming fire from combatants on the ground by the C-17 pilots using a tactical landing where the dive angle is steeper than normal combined with a faster approach speed. We land safely, unpack our bags and head over to in-processing where they tell us about the rules, mine fields, recent activity, up to date intelligence, and other base services. My first impressions.....we've, America, been there too long! This base was built not to support combat operations, but to support these corporate businesses that have snuck their way into this area of the world. Bagram Air Base (our base of operation) had been turned into a Joint Base with all the support you would find at a military base in the states, coupled with the dangers of Afghanistan.

To be clear, the entire country was not a threat to the coalition at this time. Rather, it was the terrorist network of fighters that literally entered Afghanistan to fight, die, then run back to Pakistan. I envisioned this war to look a little more rugged but at this point, its 7 years later after the first operations of the war such as Operation Anaconda. Was I too late, did I miss my chance to be a part of military history? Honestly, yes I did miss my chance! It seemed this war had been over for many years and now, it's just fighting between factions of people who are just looking for someone to fight that disagrees with them.

There are no military objectives such as the seizure of infrastructure, Destruction of Air Defense, Suppression of Air Defense, or an established opposing military force to fight against. It's just a group of disgruntled assholes looking to fight Americans. Our job there was simple, to rescue and save the lives of those who are wounded in battle in our region of Afghanistan (RC-East).

The Afghanistan war is more of a skirmish where we would leave our base, go fight, and if we didn't die, returned to base to fight again. Our missions were 24 hours a day, 7 days a week. We were split into two shifts with two crews each = 1 formation per shift. Our shifts were 12 hours long where we would sit ready on Alert until a call came in. We were the military's combat capable asset specifically trained for CSAR and Casualty Evacuations operations. We were not the primary forces for Medical Evacuations (MEDEVAC) because we did not bear the medical emblem of a Red Cross on our aircraft. Under the Geneva Convention established rules, an aircraft or personnel that wore the Red Cross on their vehicles or uniforms were not considered combatants and should not be fired upon.

Our Pavehawk aircraft was considered a lawful target because it was armed with two 50-Caliber machine guns, and each crew member carried an M-4 Carbine Rifle and an M-9 Pistol for personal/aircrew defense. Since terrorist groups (Taliban & other militia groups) did not follow the rules of war and shot at any aircraft regardless of combatant status, the military commanders insisted on CSAR support for battlefield evacuations of wounded or killed personnel. The first mission which I realized how desensitized to war, death, and destruction I have become came three weeks after arrival. We were forward deployed to a Forward Operating Base called Bostik in north-eastern Afghanistan. We were there to support combat operations to push Taliban forces back into Pakistan by driving them out. This was my first operation where we supported Army Special Forces and the Afghan Commandos who were just as high speed as their Green Beret liaisons. FOB Bostik was like many FOBs isolated with mountains that surrounded us. Not only were we there to support the main operation, we were on call to support the conventional Army Combat Outpost in the area.

One morning, we get a call that a suicide bomber detonated herself at a check point on one of the main supply routes. The call was 4 Category Alphas (highest priority, life threatening injuries), with 2 possible KIA. We rushed to our Helicopter, placed our protective gear on, started the helicopter and took off southbound in 7 mins. We arrived on scene to an explosion and a raging fire where the bomb went off.

We established contact with the ground team who provided us with coordinates for the landing zone. We landed the helicopters one at a time to pick up two patients each. Our helicopter call sign was Pedro 84. When Pedro 84 arrived to pick up the wounded and the dead, we landed as fast as possible in order to expedite the pickup. There was still a chance to save the possible KIA if we got him to the surgeon in the next 10 mins. We loaded the first patient who was conscious and looking for his buddy to make sure he's ok. When we loaded the second patient, it was clear he had passed from the concussion blast of the bomb. His eyes were lifeless and his body was motionless from when he entered the cabin. The PJ desperately provided medical treatment and CPR for the entire 4 minute flight to the nearest field hospital. We arrived at F.O.B. Wright and dropped the patients off at the field hospital, closed our doors, and returned to FOB Bostik where we never found out the status of those patients that were severely wounded.

I did however in the future, in 2019, watch a documentary on Amazon Prime where I recognized the soldier being interviewed only by the shape of his face and bone structure. I recognized the seriousness of his emotions as he told the cameraman what happened to him and his team on the day they were ambushed. There are few things I will never forget in this lifetime. One of those things is the look of a man who is realizing his friends have died and he has not. It's a shocking revelation that freezes your thoughts and actions into the moment it all changed. That was his look....that's what I remembered seeing 10 years later. I had picked this young man up on the same day he was wounded and he survived. That documentary was called "No Greater Love."

I was very happy to see the Army Specialist had survived, but it was clear that he had a long road to recovery from his injuries (both seen and unseen). We continued the rest of the deployment where we would rush out to the battlefield and save the wounded and return the fallen. This first deployment was largely uneventful but gave me a great sense of purpose to the importance of our mission, to rescue those from the battlefield, living up to the motto "That Others May Live." We rotated back home to Okinawa where I reunited with my loving wife, awesome son, and beautiful 7 month old daughter who unfortunately did not recognize me when I went to greet her, shying away to her mother while crying as I approached. That hurt, but was slowly remedied with focused love; giving to my lovely daughter who eventually remembers me as her father 30 days later. Me and my daughter have been inseparable ever since as she is the best daughter a father could ever have.

I stayed home for six months before I was sent back out to Afghanistan for my second combat rotation. But before I am sent out again, I reflect on the events of the past deployment that have imprinted on my soul; providing me with a distinctive level of readiness for the worst possible scenario. Events such as the crash of Pedro 66 (A helicopter crew stationed in the southern region of Afghanistan) where 5 out of 7 crew members were killed. We heard the news as we were sitting on CASEVAC alert in support of an Army Ranger take down of a High Value Target.

Our squadron commander (Call sign Spank) received the news through his leadership channels and briefs us on what had happened and the unknown factors at the time. He also encouraged us to maintain focus on our current operations and know that once he received more info, so will we. We all knew someone on that flight as the CSAR community is relatively small. I personally was a student during Initial Qualification Training with the Aerial Gunner (who survived) at Kirtland AFB in New Mexico.

This is indeed a small world in which our shared experiences will always be connected through triumph and pain. I wish that was the only incident in which we as a community would lose good friends in training or in combat, but sadly it will not be. Other lessons I learned from the deployment were my mistakes and improving my crew coordination with my teammates in the helicopter. I recognized my mistakes in the Aircraft during incidents which couldn't be rehearsed during training. One incident in particular was during our forward deployment to the Kunar River Valley where the 173rd Airborne Brigade was in heavy contact with the enemy. During this mission, a squad on patrol where ambushed by an unknown number of fighters with small arms and Rocket Propelled Grenades (RPG).

As the fighting died down, members of the 13 man squad ran out of water and became severely dehydrated. The team leader called for a MEDEVAC and we responded as the closest asset to the team who could provide armed support (due to the recent Troops in Contact with the enemy). The mission was to pick up about 5 category Bravos for severe dehydration and drop them off at the nearest medical facility for treatment. As we prepared to launch we received last known information concerning enemy activity as they were last seen due east of the patrols positions. We were coming from the north traveling south, and the winds were also out the south....putting the enemy on my side of the aircraft.

We launched heading south as fast as we could, talking to the team on one radio, our commander on the satellite radio, and de-confliction air traffic on another radio. At one point everyone was talking at the same time (which was typical within the area of operation).

As we flew towards the terminal area I vigorously scanned the east looking out for any movement, uniforms, weapons, concealment, puffs of smoke in an area not determined to be friendly. Searching for threats in a helicopter with your head out in the wind at 100 knots airspeed is an activity of visualization. You will NEVER hear anyone shooting at you until the bullets hit you or your aircraft. You will NEVER hear the whistle of an RPG or other surface to air missile unless it hits you. Keep in mind, this mission was during the day time, so bullets and muzzle flashes are extremely difficult to catch before it's too late. I knew these facts and did my best to find the enemy before they shot at us.

As we arrived at the Terminal area where the soldiers were, I had one hand on my machine gun, one hand togging different channels on my radios to communicate between my crew, our commander in the command center, and scanning heads out moving my gun where my eyes looked. We go over the plan on who will stay above and who will pick up the casualties. Once the plan is set we all acknowledge our respective crew positions for understanding - Pilot (Aircraft Commander), Co (Co-Pilot), Right (Flight Engineer), Left (Aerial Gunner).

Our pattern of flight is a right hand circle over the objective which kept the threat closest to my side of the aircraft. I kept my scan up and my radio communication constant during the over-head flight pattern. Then, I fucked up without knowing. While I was switching my radio toggle from channel 5 to channel 1.....I missed the channel 1...turning the dial too far to the private setting. With scanning, communicating, and trying to decipher all the comm chatter, I failed to look heads-in to see which radio I was operating on. In the Private setting, I can still hear everything the crew and what outside radio communication are saying, but my crew cannot hear me.

Unfortunately, I couldn't tell that my crew could not hear me because when I answered crew responses, I was never questioned "gunner can you hear us, we can't hear you". We practice communication failures within the crew during training but with total comm failures instead of partials. Meaning, when your comm failed, you heard nothing, not even your own voice. It's a really clear indication of being Comm Out and we communicate with Hand/Arm signals until communication is re-established. But communication works both ways. I was out, and my crew didn't hear me.....but why did they never ask? I was out for about 5 mins, still hearing everything and responding as appropriate. We make our approach to the hover where we will hoist them up to the helicopter as we cannot land in the area.

Normal communication sounds during an approach are as follows:

Co-Pilot - 100 feet at 50 Knots

Flight Engineer - Clear Forward Down Right

Aerial Gunner - Clear Forward Down Left

Pilot - flying the aircraft and listening to the calls and positions.

Abnormal Communication while I was comm out were like this:

Co-Pilot - 100 feet at 50 Knots

Flight Engineer - Clear Forward Down Right

Aerial Gunner - [Silence]

Pilot - flying the aircraft and listening to the calls and positions.

Co-Pilot - 65 feet at 20 Knots

Flight Engineer - Clear Forward Down Right

Aerial Gunner - [Silence]

Pilot - flying the aircraft and listening to the calls and positions.

Co-Pilot - 50 feet at 10 Knots

Flight Engineer - Clear Forward Down Right, come forward 10 feet

Aerial Gunner - [Silence]

Pilot - flying the aircraft and listening to the calls and positions.

We hovered over the patients for 20 mins all while still not having full communication with each other. Furthermore, It is normal to have a tree or bush close to the rotor blades so long as the crew is aware and we make the required safety calls; "Bush inside the disk at 9 o'clock, well above no factor...Stop Down Come Up 10, Well above, No Factor. On this day, I had a bush/tree that presented a risk to the helicopter on my side. I called it out to the crew telling them to Stop Down (stop descending) Come Up 10. The helicopter responds and rises above the tree. I am still comm out, but I assumed my crew can hear me.

The advisory calls continued until I noticed the crew was not responding to my calls. The helicopter descends further into the bush, closer, even closer....contact. The co-pilot screams "Gunner you don't see that fucking bush?" Light Bulb moment....I look at my comm switch and I'm on fucking private. I correct the problem and resume communications, but the rotor blades have already skimmed the bunch, causing damage to the blades.

We completed the mission and returned to the base and me and the Flight Engineer got into an argument about what happened. My defense was "how the fuck did no one hear me for 20 fucking minutes. I could've been shot dead." Their attack was "what the fuck were you doing?" This attack angered me because the assumption was that the Gunner was never doing much or had nothing to do while the rest of the crew flew the aircraft. I had just as much responsibility as the next crew member. I never entered as a "Passenger." I received a qualification downgrade because of my failure to identify the communication problem, but my Aircraft Commander also received a downgrade for not identifying the breakdown in crew coordination. Also worth noting was that the day after we had our mishap, we were all drug tested for safety reasons....oh yeah, and it was my birthday. Happy 27th Birthday....Your gift, assumption of fault by your crewmembers and the pending investigation concerning damage to Air Force property. You're welcome!

With these lessons in the back of my head, I was ready for round 2, and this time, all my training would be tested in several life and death moments that have been etched into the vast history of CSAR missions conducted by its well trained crews. Operation Strong Eagle III was the second major battle we've participated in as a CSAR crew during my deployment and was the first action I would participate in that proved how lucky you have to be in combat. The operation was once again led by the No Slack Battalion of the 327th Infantry Regiment, 101st Airborne Division.

This operation was documented in the film "The Hornet's Nest." Although the operation was complex and detailed with primary objectives for the men fighting the insurgent forces and terrorist leaders on the ground, our mission was simple. When they called, we will be there. The operations kicked off with an Air Assault that started at 3 AM launching from FOB Joyce (Near the Kunar River Valley). The entire battalion was involved with the operation to kill and disrupt the network of insurgent fighters crossing the border to Afghanistan and taking refuge in a village for offensive staging against coalition forces. Our mission was still clear, to provide CSAR support for the boots on the ground and the supporting air assets (OH-58, CH-47and AH-64 helicopters). As the operation kicks off we receive a few calls in the middle of the morning (about 4 hours in) to pick up a few category Charlies (sprained ankles, fall injuries, etc). We tried to sleep as much as possible so when the call came, it woke us up from our comma and we spirited towards our aircraft.

Our aircraft were not very close to where we slept so the run was a ways and the air was thick with dust. By the time we got to the bird and started the checklist, all you heard was us coughing over the comms to clear our throats. We get ourselves under control and take off to support the men in the fight. The first night of the operation was our first combat saves of the mission. We scramble at about 10 PM for 3 category Alpha (urgent, life threatening) wounds during the first contact with the enemy. Under night vision goggles, everything is green with a 40 degree field of vision to the wearer.

At night, you can see everything, the moon, other aircraft, and the No Slack soldiers exchanging fire with the enemy. It was an intense battle uphill to retake a compound the insurgents were using a fighting position. We circled west of the objective waiting for our chance to get in there and rescue the wounded. As we waited, we watched our fighting men and their Apache helicopter support destroy the objective in awe of the sheer power of our infantry. It was one of my most memorable moments which solidified my reason for serving…..finding the enemy & killing them. We received the clearance to pick up the wounded from a 50 foot hover as the battle raged around us in the dark of night. But the operation is not over, we still have 7 more days of fighting left.

Delta Transition

Get over yourself and complete the task given to you as if your life depended on it. Remove all forms of doubt from your mind and your vocabulary. If there is something in this world you are meant to do, simply go out there and get it done. There is no limit to what your mind and your body are capable of doing. Be the smartest person in the room, and if you are not, continue to strive to be an expert. Be the best that others call on for help. Be dependable, be flexible, and be caring to others as you may need them some day. But most of all, learn humility. Be humble about your successes and never settle for anything less than what you deserve...even if the journey is fraught with danger. Confidence and courage are learned traits that we are never born with. We must learn to be confident in yourself and build internal courage for others when we are not at our best. Be able to take constructive criticism from your peers and speak your mind when you know deeply that your point of view is important. You may be the voice that saves lives, money, time, and other resources. It is often said that there are two types of people...sheep and sheepdogs. Fuck being a sheep. Be the protector, even if the only asset you have to protect is your feelings. Be strong for others and stronger for yourself when you are at your weakest. Your bravery will be called upon by life during your transition period. Be a sheepdog when the time approaches. Being courageous is hard to maintain and will be exhausting on your life and others around you. I never steered away from the opportunity to show courage in the face of adversity. Whether that is telling my boss I don't agree, or turning down an opportunity because the cost doesn't outweigh the benefit, courage is the salt you place on a wound. It will hurt, but it will help toughen your resolve.

Transition Five:

From Someone To No one - Expect Nothing!

At this point of the deployment to Afghanistan, I had become very proud of the work we were doing within the area of responsibility (AOR), volunteering for activities that would contribute to the morale of the unit and the people we served. There was never a feeling of untouchability within the squadron, but we were getting closer to realizing we can be touched, hurt, or even worse, killed. Operation Strong Eagle III raged on for 7 more days and the missions kept coming in. One rescue from the valley floor, another over a house that was commandeered by the No Slack Battalion at night on Night Vision Goggles. But not every mission was a save, some missions were to return our fallen Heroes back to home from the battlefield in which they bravely gave their life. I cannot tell you how many servicemen and women we saved and how many we returned home. That number didn't matter to us as a crew or squadron.

The mission, the task and the objective was to rescue or recover our brothers and sisters in arms at all cost. On the third day of the operation, we continue to receive calls for more pickups...this time during the heaviest fighting of the entire operation. The casualties were starting to increase as we received a call to scramble our aircraft, preparing to pick up 1

KIA (Killed in Action) and 1 severely wounded soldier. The infantry squad were isolated and surrounded by insurgent forces that fired upon them from all sides from well covered concealment. The wounded soldier we were rushing to save had suffered a gunshot wound to his chest...time was of the essence. We launched as quickly as we could and held an airborne hold due west of the last known position of the wounded to gather more information concerning the patient and the surrounding enemy.

We used 9-Lines of information to give us as much detail about the mission within a short amount of time. Information such as location, medical injury, call-sign, number of patients etc. completed the 9-line report. The fifth line of the 9-Line read-out was "Enemy Location." I will never forget this call because it was daunting, and it was broadcasted over the Satellite radio for the entire region. Typically, when the enemy positions are identified, it's with Bearing, Range, Azimuth, and Attitude. For example "Southwest our position, two zero zero for 600 Meters, High High." On this day, the call was simple..."ENEMY FUCKING EVERYWHERE!" we knew this may be the day we would get touched by the hot sting of a fast moving bullet or be shot down in a glorious blaze of fire.

We gathered the rest of the info and communicated with the attached Assault Weapons Teams (AH-64s) to de-conflict our flight paths and Gun Target Lines. PJs received all the info they needed, the crews understood the game plan, so we proceeded to rescue and recover the wounded & KIA. We, the Pedro formation, are on our second attempt at recovering the wounded soldiers because the first MEDEVAC (Medical Evacuation Army aircraft) took direct ground fire which wounded the pilot. MEDEVAC helicopters are not configured for weapons employment and are not able to defend against the machine gun fire. This fact is on everyone's mind as we push towards location in our aircraft.

The expectation of going into battle as a Pedro is to save lives first, but we will destroy anyone who gets in our way (military legal targets). We scan the area for both our friendly forces on the ground and anyone not identified as friendly. The Rule of Engagement was "Weapons Tight" meaning we were only allowed to destroy targets that were positively identified as enemies. This was difficult because the Taliban fighters wore regular clothes and did not have any distinctive identifying insignias.

Every male in that area slung an AK-47 over their shoulder so determining the enemy meant waiting until they showed intent. Which means rounds coming our way, or the act of pointing their weapon in our direction. At this point the village locals had moved out of the area because of the fight, so anyone that was left with a weapon was considered a legal target. This is also the first year the Multi-Cam pattern uniforms were operationalized in Afghanistan by conventional forces, making it difficult to spot the soldiers with naked sight. Thankfully, this concealment made it harder for the enemy to spot our soldiers also, reducing their casualty rate. As we arrive at the last known point, we look for the survivors while scanning for enemy activity.

The fighting has been quiet, but only because the insurgent fighters were waiting for us to arrive on scene. Thankfully, we located our objective by the VS-17 panel displayed by the soldiers (orange panel which contrasted with terrain). We began our checklist to pick up the wounded first, then the KIA. The Flight Engineer and the PJs also began to prepare the hoist device which will lower the PJs from the helicopter to the ground. We approach the soldiers at a 65 foot hover (as their locations made it impossible to land the entire helicopter)....The PJs hooked up to the hoist hook and begin to swing out the door when.....RAT TATATATATATATA, we are engaged by an enemy machine gunner who waited until the PJs were at the door of the helicopter exposed and unprotected. This was the first instance of the operation in which our helicopter was hit by direct and accurate fire.

As the bullets hit our helicopter, it nearly misses the PJs and the Flight Engineer by a few inches, escaping unscathed. But we are not out of the woods yet. The shots fired were a burst (5 - 10 rounds), We only heard the bullets that impacted the helicopter, there is no way of knowing exactly how long we were engaged during the hover as it's the middle of the day. The bullets impacted the lower portion of the fuel tanks, than impacted the #2 engine (on the right side of the bird). This suggested the rise of the muzzle when being fired from a lower or equal position. Once the bullets impacted the engine, it caused a shift in power distribution causing the helicopter to descend from the hover. Our helicopter needed both engines to hover, and we just had our #2 struck with gun fire. Take a wild guess what happens next.

This entire engagement lasted about 2-3 seconds, but in those seconds the enemy was able to incapacitate our helicopter's ability to hover and rescue the survivors from the battlefield. We begin to fall out of the sky....the Pilot tells the Co-Pilot (who had control of the helicopter) " "go left, go left, go left." As we fell, I tried to swing my weapon to the rear of the helicopter, but was unable to engage targets because of friendly positions below us, and the rapid descent of the helicopter.

Falling was the best solution for the loss of engine power during a hover, here's why. Although we were 65 feet above our objective, we were 400 feet above the valley falling from a drainage on the side of the mountain. We fell fast enough that our #1 engine (the operational one) was able to provide us enough power for forward flight. This was called a Single Engine emergency, meaning the helicopter couldn't hover, but it could fly forward so long as it was going fast enough. We pull up from the dive and began our single engine climb up. All crew members were safe, but now our helicopter is screaming RED at us. All the indications associated with the #2 Engine were in the red (Turbine Gas Temperature, Engine Speed, Oil Pressure, etc.). We relayed to our trail helicopter (second in the formation) our status and new game plan, to shut down the engine in-flight and Land as Soon as Possible. I looked at the PJs and gave them hand signals, we may have to crash land if we don't make it to an established airfield. The hand signal relays the message, but not the severity as it is simply bringing my hands together (with one hand being the helicopter, and the other the ground). We as a crew prepared to land since the issue was not only that we had only one engine, but we don't know the condition of the engine internally. Anything could still occur which could make the engine have a catastrophic failure from the explosion of flammable liquids. Luckily, we were close operationally to a coalition force controlled airfield in Jalalabad. We declared an aircraft emergency which gave us clearance to land before anyone else.

We performed a text-book single engine roll-on landing on the airfield and shut the aircraft down immediately. By this time, our home Tactical Operations Center at Bagram Airbase was aware of our engagement and has generated a spare crew to relive our formation and take over the Alert status for the remainder of the operation. There is something to be said about an Army aviation mechanic who is trained and motivated to provide force multiplying aircraft to the fight. We provided our Pavehawk to the Army aviation battalion who maintained Blackhawks (same aircraft engines, different variation). They worked on our helicopter non-stop and were able (with the assistance of our Air Force maintenance team), to replace our engine with one of their 701C GE Engines; allowing us to fly our bird back to the main base for future inspection 2 days later. Sadly, Strong Eagle III would end with those soldiers we attempted to rescue dying from their wounds because of our delay. That was the first mission I was involved with that we were not able to complete our objective due to enemy fire. I think that failure reinforced our resolve to never let the enemy dictate our objectives. Come hell or high water, we will complete our mission.

TOKYO TOKYO TOKYO: We are on CSAR alert from Bagram Air Base which started just as normally as all shifts before. There are two calls we receive over the radio and through "vocal cords" when we get a particular mission. REDCON refers to a MEDEVAC mission (light to no threat, personnel only). TOKYO refers to a downed aircraft (medium to high threat). For response times, REDCON calls have different condition levels which dictates how fast we need to launch. For most REDCON calls we have no more to 30 minutes to launch from notification. TOKYO calls are more urgent, launching is required (wheels off the ground) within 15 minutes.

I remember being in the Ready Room looking at a show on television, reading a magazine, or talking to my teammates about dumb shit. Loudly, with a sense of urgency, our Flight Lead (J. Hallada) yells TOKYO TOKYO TOKYO! We all dropped whatever we were doing as it immediately was not important. Talking to your spouse, playing a game, completing coursework, nothing matters when the call for a TOKYO comes from the Tactical Operations Center (TOC). We ran to the TOC to get the updates on the current situation. It's an Army OH-58 Kiowa helicopter, crew of two, call-sign Pest 55, wingman Pest 56, location: Alazay Valley, status: 1 KIA, 1 Ambulatory, Enemy: unknown.

As far as we can tell from initial intelligence, the helicopter crashed in an area for unknown reasons. One pilot is dead, the other is alive (making the radio call to his wingman for help). We gathered up for a quick mission brief which took 1 minute, then we ran to our helicopters to prepare our gear and start up the bird. This was my first actual Tokyo call in which we were conducting Combat Search and Rescue operations in accordance with our doctrine. We trained for this scenario for days, months, years..... hours upon hours of flying. Always ready for the call to come, stating "we got a bird down in enemy territory...go get them and bring them home." It was exhilarating, exciting, and heart-pounding. Of all things, it was not scary. There was no fear of the unknown or the possibility of failure.

Someone was having their worst day...it was time for us to have our best! This was the big show, possibly the mission that would be talked about and studied for years. Little did I know, I was right. But will I be able to perform? Will I do my best, will I make my crew proud? My Fight Engineer (J. Davis) had told me during a prior bullshit session about his previous deployments to Iraq. I can't for the life of me remember where this story came from, but he told me that during a mission, his aircraft was engaged by a Man-Portable Anti-Aircraft Device (MANPAD). This was a shoulder launched infra-red missile that can be launched by a single individual. I may have slipped about my fears concerning not performing well. I had not been tested in my opinion in a tough scenario.

I wanted to know what I was made of. He told me when they were engaged, the Aerial Gunner froze in his crew position and did not react. No calls, no countermeasures giving, not returning fire. His lesson to me was don't freeze like he did. When the time comes, act, do, and respond. I never forgot that conversation and ensured that when the time presented itself, I would not disappoint him. After all, he only was one of my instructors during initial qualification training. From an instructor during training, to now as my crewmember in combat, he was just as cool. Always calm and logical, J. Davis never let the small shit get to him. There were too many important things to worry about during flight than the politics of the world. He was also a highly experienced Flight Engineer who ran out of fucks to give to anyone else. Hell, he once took a shit in an ammunition can during a flight in Iraq and flew with the can the whole mission until completion. We've smelled worse in our helicopter but never from our own doing. I trusted this man and I needed him to trust that I will do my duty when called upon. Where there is action to be held during every deployment of military conflict, so is there boredom to be handed out to every military participant. To me personally, every day was exciting for the simple fact that we are participating in history. We are on the right side of good and we will be remembered for stepping up when our country was under attack during my generation's Pearl Harbor.

Others chose to use our military time to frankly act like "bitches" complaining about every little fucking detail that was not up to their unmatched standards of quality. These individuals (whomever) would complain about the food we ate to the smell of the environment we stayed in. These tensions would boil over and cause dumb-ass arguments and disputes between grown men and women who considered themselves warriors of our nation. I swear some of the time we had could've been spent just reading or getting to know each other better, but the most senior and frankly bitter enlisted members of our team found something to complain about. The expectation is to clean up after yourself and keep the fridge stocked with drinks for the next shift. This did not happen and we wound up having a sit down where members talked about their gripes with one another in the hope of finding resolution. My contribution to this meeting (which took place 3 days before the Tokyo call) was "we should not be having this debate, it is easy to just take care of each other." Then I infamously said "it could always be worse."

We launched to rescue the Pest 55 crew at 0440 in the morning. As we are enroute to the terminal area, we receive more information from our Operation Center as relayed from Pest 56. Luckily, the crash site was only about a 20 min flight which gave us the capability to rescue the wounded pilot and return him to care within 15 minutes. As we continue towards the area it is dark and we approached using our night vision equipment, but the sun will rise soon which means the NVG comes off. This was called "Pinky" time, the exact moment to come off NVGs was up to the individual crew member. As we approach the area the sun begins to rise and we establish communication with Pest 56 who has been protecting Pest 55 until we arrived. We get eyes on the crash site....it looks bad.

The helicopter is rolled over on its side and we see the dead pilot slumped over as if being pulled out from the bird. The Co-Pilot attempted to recover the body of his pilot but couldn't as he was also injured. Additionally, the pilot had already died at this point. We also saw the Co-Pilot displaced from the bird about 200 feet above the crash site as he had climbed to higher ground to avoid enemy contact and established communications with responding aircraft. With the objectives being split, we decided to infill PJs at the downed aircraft from our helicopter (Pedro 84) and to infill PJs from the lead aircraft (Pedro 83) to the surviving pilot. My bird was the second aircraft in the formation, but was always the first to go into "the zone" to pick up the patients. As this day was no different, Pedro 84 prepared to infill the PJs via the aircraft hoist to the crash site and extricate the pilot and determine if we could be saved. Game plan is set, one's ready, two's ready, PJs ready. Execute.....two's in!

We began our approach over the crash while our PJs and Flight Engineer prepared for the 70 foot hoist down to the deceased pilot. All crew calls are made and we begin to slow to a hover over the area. 3.....2......1......stop forward, hold your hover, PJ's are out the door on their way down. As we sit in the hover, I scan for any threats or people moving other than our team and the pilots. My sight picture is surrounded by mountains and a patch of high grass and dirt to the 11 o'clock of the helicopter. PJs are down and releasing the hook of the hoist. Still no activity Left or Right. The Flight Engineer reels in the hoist to and begins to clear us for forward flight when a burst of machine gun fire strikes our aircraft from the right side. This was different from our previous engagements because you can hear the wiz of the bullets entering our open down and exiting our closed door on the left side. It's louder than before, harder hitting, and continuous.

They are shooting at the Flight Engineer. As with the previous engagements, I can't reach my machine gun around to support the right side of the aircraft as it is locked to the left. There was nothing I could do to effectively return fire, so I improvised. There was nothing and no one on my side of the helicopter so I fired 5 rounds down at my 10 o'clock as a deterrent for the enemy to stop firing at us. While I fired a quick burst of distractionary fire, J. Davis is screaming "GO GO GO GET THE FUCK OUT OF HERE." We climbed up above the crash site and established formation with our Lead aircraft to figure out where the enemy was and how we would pick-up the pilots and protect our PJs. No more than 10 seconds after the climb to safety, J. Davis tells the crew "I'm hit and I'm bleeding pretty good." In combat, there is no reason to turn your head around to look at the crew members behind you.

We communicate through our inter-comm switch while continuing to fly, calculate, scan, fire weapons, and navigate. Turning around to look over my left shoulder to see the condition J. Davis was in, I looked to find him leaned over on his left side in his crew chair with a pool, literally a pool of blood under him flowing to the rear of the cabin. The pilot radios to me, "Guns, how is he?" Gonna check him out now....Gunner's out of his crew position. But before I give assistance to my wounded crew member, the Co-Pilot (L. Nolting) tells me to lock my gun forward and takes control of it from the front for fixed forward fire (should we need it). There was a reason we trained as hard as we did, all those hours we flew, all those tactics we practiced, and all those small unit tactics movements we perfected.

Because when our helicopter goes down from enemy fire, we are now infantrymen evading capture from the enemy at all cost. We knew this possibility and carried a tactical load-out for such an occasion. My load-out consisted of my M-4 Rifle with 210 rounds of 5.56 mm (millimeter) ammunition, M-9 Pistol with 45 rounds of 9 mm, 2 MK-18 Smoke Grenades, Infrared Chem-lights, Combat Knife, two tourniquets, rescue hook knife, my body armor with survival equipment weighing 50 lbs. alone, and a camel pack 2 liters of water. All together I carried 70 extra pounds of equipment on my body for every mission.

I had become so used to the extra weight that I became very mobile with it on as I performed my duties. Getting to J. Davis took nothing out of me as he needed help. I moved over to his position to assess him. The blood was coming from his leg as detailed by his tan flight suit which was mostly saturated in that area. I laid him back and lifted up his pant leg while telling the pilots what I saw. J. Davis (Jim) screams from the pain so loud that I can hear it over the roar of the helicopter.

He was hurting, I had to work fast to stop his bleeding. I informed the pilots he's lost too much blood to continue flying and we needed to get him to a hospital as fast as possible. We are down one crew member. Both pilots acknowledged and told the lead aircraft we are heading back to base to get the Flight Engineer to the role-3 hospital. The pilots broke off and started heading back to base, hauling ass pulling as much power as they can. As I look for Jim's tourniquet on his body, I also can't find his medical kit. Dammit Jim where the fuck is your kit? Jim placed his medical kit on his backside for comfort, not for functionality as he, nor could I reach his kit easily when our motor skills went out the window. As I go to roll Jim over, he hands me his tourniquet with his shaky left hand. The son of a bitch was still in the fight as badly hurt as he was.

I grab it from him and place it far up above his bullet hole, which had turned his leg in to mess, exposing his damaged/mangled muscles covered in dark maroon colored blood. Everything I'm about to do to him will cause more pain as we raced back to base 500 feet in the air. "12 Minutes out Gonzo" the pilot yells to me. "12 minutes", I repeat back as I begin to tighten Jim's tourniquet using all my strength to make it tight enough to stop the bleeding. I crank down as hard as I can until I can't anymore, securing the tourniquet in place. I would later find out that Jim has lost about 3 liters of blood when the human body holds over 5 liters.

With the tourniquet in place, I rummage through the PJs medical kit to look for gauze or an Israeli bandage to cover his wound. Not knowing the layout of the bags it took me longer than I wanted and I grabbed the first thing I could find that was close (Quikclot gauze). I used this to wrap Jim's leg up to help absorb the blood and cover the hole. Hindsight 20/20 this was not the worst method of covering up the wound and I would be haunted for many years after this incident feeling like I fucked up or I didn't do enough of a good job. As I knew this dressing was not sufficient, I elevated Jim's leg above my left shoulder and held his would close with my hands holding his leg together for the next 10 minutes. Without giving it a second thought as to what I was doing, from the outside looking in, I was covered in blood, on my knees with the wind blowing vigorously, surrounded by mountains in a loud screaming helicopter soaring above an active battlefield.

While we were heading back, the other Lead helicopter was still engaged with the enemy combatants shooting at the PJs and the surviving pilot. We had to make it back to them fast as we are still largely isolated from other friendly forces as they are not aware yet. Parts of my tan flight suit will stay covered in blood as we had no time to change, nor did we really give a shit. As I continued to care for my crew member and friend, I would watch the life slip from his eye every 3 - 4 minutes. This scared the living hell out of me, please don't fucking die, holy shit don't fucking die. As Jim's movement would stop and he would close his eyes as if trying to fall asleep, I would slap the living shit out of him and scream "WAKE UP JIM, WAKE THE FUCK UP". I knew his pain was great and the slap across his helmet would not cause any more, but it did cause him to open his eyes and stay with me. Every time he closed his eyes, my hand met the side of his helmet.

I didn't want him to get comfortable, we were almost there to the hospital, Fight Motherfucker, Fight! Finally, we get to Bagram Air Base where we declare an emergency and hover taxi to hospital drop off point. Of course we called the radio operators at the hospital telling them we were inbound with an urgent surgical patient, hoping that they would be ready for us when we pulled up to the fence.......nope. We arrived and no medical personnel there to meet us. We continued to call them over the radio telling them we are here, please send out a stretcher. This was about 90 seconds of waiting, but it felt like an eternity. Fuck it, we decided collectively, we'll bring him in ourselves. So many things we could've done differently or better but in the heat of the moment, we just did. The Co-Pilot hopes out of his seat and leaves the Pilot with the controls alone.

The Pilot in Command (Major Bryant) was a 120% competent pilot and had thousands of hours flying, so leaving him in a zero threat environment alone on the sticks was nothing. Me and the Co-Pilot decided to carry Jim to the hospital which was 150 meters away. If I could provide a visual depiction of Jim, he is 6 feet tall and weighs about 220 pounds. With all of his equipment, he was close to 280. Speed was our goal as he was very close to falling further into unconsciousness. The Co-Pilot grabbed his leg and I grabbed his chest by interlocking my fingers. Pulling him to the door caused him more pain which I hated doing, but it also proved that he was still alive and breathing. We began to carry him to the hospital and it was the most physically exhausting task we both had ever taken because not only did Jim have all of his gear on, so did we.

We struggled to move him fast, but luckily, a Marine lieutenant saw us carrying our bloodied friend and ran over to help us further carry Jim to the hospital. We bust through the Emergency Room doors and scream we need help, and the doctors rushed to our aid with a stretcher and took Jim for immediate surgery. We give the Doctors a briefing of what happened to us and the extent of his injuries to the best of our knowledge. Then we say our quick goodbyes and tell Jim we'll see him later. By this time, he is out cold so he doesn't hear anything we say. We ran back to our helicopter where we still had a mission to do, rescue the pilots, support our Lead aircraft, and protect the PJs.

We taxi to the fuel pit to get some more gas and perform a Battle Damage Assessment of the helicopter. We are looking for smoke, fire, vibrations, and equipment clearly not operating correctly. The BDA check is good and we determined we can still fly the helicopter. We called our commander in the TOC to give him an update of the situation. We also headed back to the squadron area to pick up a new crew member, call-sign Scuba (who had been woken up during his sleep), to replace Jim. We pick him up and give him the details of the operation. He acknowledges, takes his seat, and prepares for flight. The poor bastard had to sit in the same seat where Jim was just hit, with all the damage from the bullets still present, and Jim's blood still pooled on the cabin floor. We didn't have time to clean the cabin so when Scuba asked "whose blood is this?" It's Jim's I replied, but he'll be ok, he's in surgery.

The Pilot asked "Is everybody ready?" Without any preservation, we all answered with our crew positions and acknowledged we were ready - Co, Right, Left. We taxi and take off back to the battlefield where we would spend the next 4.5 hours attempting to complete our mission. That untouchable feeling slowly faded as the mission persisted forwarded. Today may be the day we die in a fiery blaze of glory. I've never been this scared in my whole life to where I could feel it all over my body. But the biggest fear is not performing and doing your job. Everything else is bullshit. Do your job and die if you have to, but do your damn job. Your crew needed you. My crew needed me.

We trucked back out to the crash site where by this time the whole fucking country knew what was happening. There was an aircraft down and it was proving difficult to reduce them. So what does the US military do, they throw everything they can at it! This was great but also caused some problems as every commander wanted a piece of this rescue. So what did they send us......2 A-10s, 2 F-15s, 1 CH-47 Quick Reaction Force with a Platoon of Infantry, and 2 AH-64s. All those air and ground assets were a comfort for us, but it over-crowded the battle space which was a valley called the Alazay.

As we headed back to meet up with Pedro 83 (who had been fighting alone for about 40 minutes) they were on their way back to Bagram due to rescuing the surviving pilot, but also because of excessive battle damage that caused their transmission system to leak all of its oil. We entered the battle space to make contact with our PJs on the ground who are lower than snake shit trying to avoid the incoming fire from the enemy (at this point, we still don't know who the fuck is shooting at us).

We had the AH-64 saturate the area as much as possible before we made another approach to the area. The PJs had been battling for almost 70 minutes alone trying to figure out how to retrieve the dead pilot from the helicopter. Every attempt they made was thwarted with heavy machine gun fire. The game plan for us was simple and the same as it always was. But there was so much resistance this day that it almost became impossible to retrieve the pilot. We would make multiple attempts when we received the clearance from the other aircraft for de-confliction.

We wouldn't want them shooting as we made our approach, getting caught in a crossfire. We made the attempt and just like that, we are shot off the landing zone again........and again..........and again. We are shot at with direct and accurate fire which is still to this day the loudest noise I have ever experienced. It's nothing like you watch on television or through the safety of your mobile device. It will always make you jump and look for where the fire is coming from when you're at your angriest, wanting to kill something. Everyone in the formation took some damage to their protective equipment which saved our lives too during that mission.

Scuba was shot through his fucking helmet, which thankfully, did not go through his head.

The other Flight Engineer in the Lead helicopter, Mike Price, was shot through the back of his seat, but thankfully, his MK-18 Smoke Grenade absorbed the bullet, preserving it for him to see at the end of the flight. Had that not been there, he would've been killed by being shot in the back just barely below his body armor. I myself had a bullet penetrate the helicopter from below my seat missing my nuts as I was sitting on one knee.

The bullet came from under me and broke off in two pieces. One piece bounced off my left knee (with no penetration, just force) and the other piece hit the flight control rods causing them to bend, but continue operating. When the bullet from under me struck, I immediately tasted the brass and other metals which penetrated my taste buds so sharply, that it felt like I was chewing on hot, spent bullets. The mission continued and we desperately tried to find an IN to exploit to rescue the dead pilot. At one point, the enemy continued to fire upon the downed helicopter which caused it to catch fire.

This was tough on the PJs and the crew because his body was being burned and we had no fire extinguishing equipment. The pilot's body would continue to burn for the rest of the morning. We keep trying, regardless of the circumstances to rescue the pilot from this deteriorating battlefield. We needed help and reinforcements. The Quick Reaction Force from a nearby base finally arrives on the battlefield with a platoon (about 30 men) of battle hardened soldiers who wanted to help our situation. We watched the CH-47 land in between us, the enemy, and the crash site to form a blocking pattern. This created a fatal funnel for the off-loading soldiers who were targeted as they rapidly off-loaded the helicopter. This initial fire caused 2 immediate casualties, their medic was killed, and another fire team member was shot through his chest. In an instant, we now have to rescue the deceased pilot, recover the killed medic, and rescue the injured infantryman who were separated by 300 yards in the middle of a firefight between us and an unknown number of enemy fighters. Getting low on fuel, we head to a nearby FOB to get some gas and to pick up some ammo for the QRF who were running low.

As we shut down the aircraft and perform another battle damage assessment, it dawns on us how much damage we actually took. Keep in mind, the battle is still not over and we will be heading back there in a few minutes. It is during this BDA check that I noticed the bullet that narrowly missed my testicles that exploded upon impact causing me to taste the brass. I informed my crew member Scuba who showed me the bullet hole in his helmet. We complete our checks and determine we can still fly. Just then, my counterpart (Justin Tite) in the Lead's new aircraft came over to me to check on how I was doing. I told him, I'm fine and just hopes that Jim is OK.

Then, I start to cry as it all hits me what just happened and what is still happening. I cry for 5 seconds, wiping my tears as I tell Justin "at least Jim can skip his physical fitness test, he didn't wanna do that shit anyway!" We both begin to laugh as it was comforting for both of us that we can still make jokes in light of not knowing what Jim's condition was. Was his Ok? Was he still alive? After we return to our aircraft and perform our take-off checklist, we complete another crew briefing where the objective is to recover the pilot, recover the killed medic, and rescue the critically wounded QRF Member. At this point, the Lead aircraft had picked up the rest of the PJ team from Bagram AB to support the PJs on the ground in the valley anyway they could. 2 PJs get on our bird and head back with us into the fight. As I sit in my seat, I feel like the likelihood of dying today is high. I pull out my pistol, place a round in the chamber, and holster it. Time to become a hard target, everything I learned may be tested today. My shooting skills, my fighting skills, my evasion tactics, and my fitness is on the line. As we fly back to the valley where all the air assets are continuing to saturate the area of enemy combatants and protect the Americans on the ground, the winds change and we shift our pattern to the opposite direction. This places the threat area on my side only and allows the flight engineer to perform hoist operations.

The game plan this time was to perform a simultaneous pick up of both the deceased pilot, and pick up the QRF team members. With the Apache helicopters (AH-64s) and other assets above head, we were tactically allowed to perform this maneuver. The Trail bird would rescue the QRF members, the Lead bird would recover the pilot from the crashed helicopter. We execute on final approach calling out airspeed and altitude. I'm heads out of my window scanning for enemy positions, I look down at both the QRF in their fighting positions and I can see clearly that they are being engaged from a building that is about 150 meters away from our position.

The impact from their bullets kicking up the mud from the building creates a clear unnatural puff of dust. That fucking building has to go and everyone in it, who is using it for cover, are my target. I call out "ground fire, 9 o'clock" as we reach our altitude over the objective. I return fire with a burst of 5 bullets, but they miss as we have descended lower than the building and I was unable to fire my machine gun that high, or else I could hit my rotor blades. I tell the pilots to come up 20, and as they start to climb they make the determination to go around and try again.

As we climbed back up to fly around again, we reached an effective altitude to engage and I started to suppress the enemy positions. We train every day to be able to fire while flying, adjusting our bullets to either trail or lead the target. As we fly forward I continue to fire on the building, completely decimating the outside and whoever was inside of it firing at our teams on the ground. The bullets we fired out the 50 caliber machine gun are explosive, armor-piercing, & incendiary rounds which looks like a firework show when they strike a target. As I fired my weapon, I see a 100 foot tree cut down by my bullets and falling over as I rain hate down on the enemy. Also, in the corner of my eye, I catch a glimpse of the coolest sight picture....the PJs were next to me firing at my target with their M-4s with a look of sheer grit and determination.

It was a glorious memory that I will never forget. We came back around to try it again (for the 7th attempt of the day), we hover in our positions over the patients and all is going well...but then, my co-pilot and I spot a flash from our 11 o'clock position. It was clear to him as he directly saw the flash and the position. To me...I was scanning to my 8 to 9 o'clock and caught the flash in my peripheral vision. My co-pilot called out to me the position which was another window. I call "Tally" and fired at the position with about 30 rounds. We destroyed that target as we flew out and around to try to make the pick up again.

My co-pilot, sensing that I was firing a lot, told me to watch my ammo and save some just in case. I replied "I have plenty." "Copy that" he responds. We carry 600 rounds of 50 Caliber ammunition for our weapons and at this point, I've only expended about less than 150 rounds. Accuracy and conservation is the name of the game. Don't shoot until you know you can destroy the target. Remember, these bullets are explosive and cause damage to any object within 5 meters of its impact.

With the enemy position destroyed by myself and the Apache helicopter flying above us, we fly in for one last approach, but this time we switch objectives. We were to retrieve the pilot and the PJs protecting him, who by this time had extricated his body out of the helicopter, but not before he was completely burned beyond recognition. We complete our approach to a hover above the crash site keeping the enemy threat to my side.

I was ready and scanning for any pop up threat as I can see the damage from the last strongholds we received fire from. Scuba lets the hoist down into the crash site for the PJs to hook up with the deceased pilot. We sit and communicate as a crew..."Hoist is on the ground"..."PJs working on Jack (code name)"..."PJs are coming up." Contrary to what you're reading, this was not a fast process and took almost 12 minutes to complete, which felt like an eternity in combat. 12 minutes for the enemy to acquire you, 12 minutes for the rounds to start hitting the helicopter and even you, 12 minutes for someone else to get hurt or killed. But the follow-on attacks never came.

We successfully suppressed the enemy either to retreat or death. We loaded our patient and PJs and called the Lead aircraft to let them know we were ready to depart back to base. Once Lead completed their mission, we called "popcorn" and returned to base where we dropped off our patients to the hospital, then to the morgue, where we wrapped our hero's body in an American flag and performed a dignified transfer from our helicopter to the medical personnel. 5 ½ hours later, our mission was complete, but at what costs? Our deployment would last an additional 3 months, and we would return back to the valley once more to rescue more soldiers with no resistance to our helicopters.....because they knew what would happen to them.

The deployment successfully ended and we returned back to our home station of Kadena AB in Okinawa Japan where for the first time we were met by our other fellow squadron airman who only heard what we did and went through together. Our mission was spread throughout the community of other CSAR squadrons in the Air Force and the Special Operations community. Going through what we went through, I expected to have my upward progression be a reflection of our combined operational success. I expected respect from my other colleagues who told me I was not ready. I expected opportunities to become an instructor when others told me I still had a lot to learn. I expected to be respected for my abilities, and not because I would drink with the fellas on weekends.

But none of those accolades came to me. None of those opportunities presented itself, and I remained in the same positions without the opportunity to progress as an instructor, as a respected crewmember, a strong team player, and as someone who was needed. This lack of change after almost dying for my brothers and sisters in Arms as well as our great country never sat well with me. But being younger at the time, I expected too much. Years of maturity as well as the exposure to traumatic events taught me to just be humble and grateful I didn't get killed, because so many others had. I completed one more combat deployment to Europe in support of special operations in North Africa before I decided.......it was time to separate from active duty. I have done may part for my country and have defended its freedom from aggression world-wide. I have placed my life on the line happily in defense of her great principles with the best men and women she has to offer. My service and my mission was complete. But I didn't want to just make a clean break as transitioning is very hard. So I decided to enlist in the National Guard for six years to wean me off the overwhelming support of active duty service. My plan was to return to New York to be closer to my family, work for law enforcement, and go to school full-time to receive my Master's degree. But as you will read......nothing with my transition into civilian life went according to plan.

Echo Transition

Never expect to get what you give. Placing yourself in situations where you are expected to be rewarded for your actions can lead to heartache when such reward never arrives. Instead, do what makes you happy to do for others. The rewards will flow your way naturally and be just as deserving. Be a better citizen, be a helpful neighbor, don't violate known laws...and if you don't know the law, find out. Be the person that is dependable not for everyone else...but for yourself and your family. My wife always tells me "waste not, want not." I'm telling you, don't waste your talents on people who do not want you. When you see clear indication that you are not valued, not wanted, or not needed, leave it. You are always important to someone and something else. Find where you fit it and go for it. Be happy to be wanted by those who appreciate your contribution to your organization or society. It will become clear when your skills are not needed. Bow out gracefully and thank them for your service. Move on efficiently with a plan or reach out to someone who has been where you are now and where you want to be. Know your value...even when others do not.

Transition Six:

From Clarity To Fog - <u>What am I even doing!</u>

The plan for transition back to civilian life after being out of it for almost 12 years seemed simple. I was at the point in my military career where I didn't feel like I was accomplishing the mission I set out to do anymore; you know, the reason that caused me to join the military in the first place. I was deployed to Afghanistan when Osama Bin Laden was killed in 2011. When we heard the news, I felt a great deal of pride because I was a part of the military at the time the #1 terrorist in the world, who caused unimaginable destruction to my city......was finally dead.

Finally, we got him...and in some small way, I was a part of it. Everything in war is connected somehow from the lowest Airman, Soldier, Sailor, Marine, Coast Guardsman, to the highest General & toughest military operation. Everything is done with a purpose and to support the larger military objective. I felt like the war could end and I've reached the end without a scratch on me....only a few close calls. When you watch the news and see the operations continued till this day, I knew it would never stop.

There always was another objective outside of my original goal of military payback for the events of 9/11. I didn't know what it was while I was serving...and frankly I didn't care much. My mission of serving my country during a time of war was complete. This was solidified when my last combat deployment was to Sicily Italy. We supported Special Operations in Northern Africa, and for the most part, were never utilized for our combat capability. It was a great experience, but fell further and further away from my personal objective towards military service. In 2013 upon the return from my deployment, I was still professionally in a place where I felt I was not advancing as fast or commensurate with my skill and capability. The arrows of decision were pointing towards the door of separation as I wasn't committed to further active duty military service.

Major combat operations have deteriorated and the focus was shifting towards the political satisfaction of members who never served a day in their fucking lives. Time to pull chocks and leave my Air Force active duty career. I decided to join the Air National Guard in Syracuse NY where I hoped to obtain a commission to be an Air Force Officer. Specifically, an Air Liaison Officer for the Tactical Air Control Party career field. While I assumed that a transfer to the National Guard would result in a speedy commissioning process, I was dead wrong. It turns out, the waiting period for commissioning took at least a year to ensure the candidate is physically and mentally prepared.

This made sense at the time, but when I decided to transfer from active duty, I was under the wrong impressions. My impression was that my commission was guaranteed based on my application. With this not being the case, I grew frustrated as I had separated from Active Duty thinking my commission was assured. This was not true. To pour salt into an open wound, the unit I applied to treated me to the same professional ridicule as my active duty counterparts. I was treated (by the enlisted members) like I was not needed or wanted in the unit. This is understandable as many people apply for these careers but quit because they can't hack it. I knew nothing was easy and would be given to me so I worked hard to just be a sponge and learn whatever I could. During the same period, I had applied to become a New York State Trooper in 2013. I was selected to take the exam, and when I passed the exam with a 95% (plus 10 points for Veteran Preference), I grew overly excited at the opportunities ahead of me in Law Enforcement and being close to my family in New York City. In 2014 (6 months before I separated), I went to Albany NY to take the fitness assessment, drug screen, and other associated tests for employment consideration. I had passed everything up to this point with flying colors shoring my commitment to military separation. Here was the largest mistake that I made and never made again in my adult future. I separated from my Active Duty status without having a job that was secured or firm.

Although I believed in my heart of hearts that I was assured employment as a NY State Trooper, this sadly was not the case. When it came to my background check, and polygraph, I was found not suitable for employment and told I could NEVER apply again for any positions in the future. What the FUCK did I just do? To make matters worse, I received the "Fuck you, you're out" 1 month after I separated. Now I am separated with no job, collecting unemployment and pondering how I will take care of my family. Fortunately for me, my years of military experience taught me to always plan for contingencies. I had three plans for my separations to ensure redundancy in case one or more plans fell apart. My plan to become a NY State Trooper was scrapped (plan A)....the plan to get my commission was scrapped (plan B).....but my final plan was to return to New York as a full-time student and utilize my GI Bill benefit.

This benefit would pay me a monthly allowance and my tuition for going to school full-time in the amount of $3744.00 a month. Combined with a part time job (in anything), I would have enough funds to cover the expenses for my family in Georgia while sleeping at my father's house. Luckily, I received a call from John Jay College of Criminal Justice informing me that I have been accepted for their Master's program in Public Administration. This was the best news I could've received because I was out of monetary options, and my savings were quickly running out. I've never depended on luck to be on my side, but throughout my life, I have always had a string of lucky instances that have kept me safe, fed, paid, and in some cases...alive. My good fortune goes way back to when I was a baby, less than a year old. In 2020, I recently met up with my cousin and his father (my Uncle) whom I haven't seen in so many years. My uncle Fredrick (who we called Uncle Fudge) told me about a time where he noticed how lucky I could really be.

My mother, as witnessed by my uncle, left me apparently alone on a second floor balcony. Homes back in the 80's did not have solid walled balconies, but they had bars or pillars that a small child can slip through. Well....my uncle watched me crawl to the edge of the balcony my mother left me alone on, and I fell. But I did not get hurt. Instead, my uncle told me he watched me float from the balcony to the ground. He watched me float 2 stories helplessly as a worried uncle would. But he saw no damage happen to me as hit the ground. In fact, he tells me I landed on my butt upright like nothing happened. I've never known my uncle to lie to me for an absurd reason to make a point or to make me feel good. Telling him about my near bouts with death spark this memory from so many years ago.

This was the last miracle story I heard in a long history of questioning my luck in life. There are so many times I felt like I should have died or been killed later in life because of deep depression, but didn't. When I was living with my father (around age 12), I would play in the hallways of my building with either a basketball to practice my dribbling skills, or a bike to perfect popping a wheely. There was a steam-heat radiator used to keep the hallway warm during the cold winter months that I would use to just sit on and rest. One day, I sat down and looked behind the radiator as if I would find something cool that someone else dropped. But I did find something today, I found a pistol. Me being a street child with plenty of sense & street knowledge, I knew not to touch it as I didn't want to imprint my fingerprints on it. But what did I do instead, I told the whole fucking neighborhood of kids outside playing games like skelly and tag. "Yo come see what I found in my building, I found a gun." I told David, Jesse, and Leslie who were all on the block at that time.

We were all intrigued as we had never seen a gun in real life before. Side Track, what the hell were we ever thinking and how fucking bored were we as kids that a pistol (revolver) was exiting enough for us to fuck with? Riddle me that Rhonda? Like most kids, we knew not to touch the damn thing, but to just look at it as it laid there. Not Leslie though, this motherfucker proceeded to grab the gun because he was sure that it wasn't real. "That shit is a fake, it's a fucking toy." We are all telling him that shit is not a toy, its fucking real. We know what toy guns look like as we all probably have one. "Nah son, this shit is fake....look." This motherfucka points the fucking gun at my fucking face with a grip that screams no firearm safety in mind, finger on the trigger, trying to squeeze. I dodge and weave pleading "stop that, I can see the bullet, it's not a fucking toy yo!" I could see the bullet pointing right at me between my eyes as Leslie, that fucking idiot, tracks my movement.

But it never fires, and that stupid asshole places the gun back where he got it. And just like that, we go about our day playing outside with each other like nothing happened. This was normal Bronx kids shit that we would experience every day. From staying out late and watching two grown men fight in the school yard at 11PM at night, to almost being jumped by the neighborhood gang because I was messing around with one of their member's girlfriends. Transitioning from Active Duty to being a civilian felt like it would be an easy challenge for me to accomplish. This was far from the truth and I have spent the rest of my adult days mentoring others from making the same mistakes I have.

Choosing a career after the military was fraught with confusion and an unclear path towards what I was meant to do. In fact, I still had no clue what I was going to be when I finally separated or retired from the Air Force. I looked back at my career and noticed that I had completed a lot of everything when it came to the competencies in Emergency Management. I thrived in an environment where there was a need for calmness during calamity. I wanted to be the person with all the answers when everyone else was freaking out. Emergency Management was the jack of all trades and master of none career field that I was meant to be a part of. But short of being in an actual job with the title of Emergency manager, I had no direct experience with the job title. I had Logistics, Aviation, security, search & rescue experience at the time of my separations. My level of experience propelled me forward into this career as I've spent the last 12 years just trying everything out. Now it was time to be the expert I've always desired to be.

The first step...use my GI Bill to obtain a Master's degree in Emergency Management as I have completed a Bachelors in Criminal Justice and Associates Degrees in Aviation &

Logistics. Sometimes your path is not a clear shot from one end to the other. My experiences provided me the ingredients to make a great meal to make from scratch. So I enrolled as a full-time student for my Masters in Public Administration with the hopes that I would land the Emergency Management job of a lifetime. School provided me and my family with an income as they were still living in Georgia which has a lower cost of living than New York City. My choice to attend school in NY was not only for the educational opportunities, but it was for the high housing allowance that I could use to supplement my income as I did not have a job upon separating. At the time, NYC paid veterans $3744.00 dollars to go to school. I just stayed at my father's house in the Bronx for the first year while I attended school and earned the housing allowance. But I still needed a job.....what was I to do?

Beware of employers that call you first without provocation or warning, for they are up to something. These employers are usually out for themselves and will use you as a warm body to achieve their financial agenda. But I was young and naive with very little guidance on how to navigate life outside of military structure and support. So when an Insurance Company cold called me because they found my resume online, I was glad and excited that someone wanted me to work with them. This was a large factor in me leaving the military, I didn't feel wanted or needed and it was good to have a company call me saying they wanted me for an interview. I set up the date and interviewed for my very first career after military service as a Life Insurance Agent. But what do I know about selling anything.

I have never been a good seller of things and I didn't have a natural knack for sales. But the prospect and the freedom provided to me for selling life insurance was a gift. I was a full-time student which was considered 4 courses during a semester. I went to school at night and I would attempt to sell insurance during the day. The clients and the company had a good model for selling their product. But if you don't have the capability or the skill to sell Ice to an Eskimo, the job can become very difficult. Fortunately, my full-time enrollment at a New York City school provided me with enough money for my family in Georgia.

Although I loved the opportunity to essentially run my own business, which includes setting my schedule, talking to potential clients, understanding self-employment operations, the benefit to cost we're never in-line for productive profitable work. This experience was invaluable for my future aspirations of starting my own business because even with no success or large profits, I enjoyed the business of operating my own business. But after 3 months of attempting to sell insurance to families, I was only able to make $700 dollars from one sale. Which is great money for the work, but because I seriously lacked the skill for selling my product (that I truly believed in), I was not able to make any serious money. So I made the decision to quit the company and focus on my studies. I would later work for the school as a Veteran Affairs student representative that paid me $8 an hour for 15 hours a week.

I have been separated from the full-time military for 4 months, and I've lost 2 jobs in 4 months. It's not looking good for me so far. The first year of my graduate school studies was largely unaffected by my ability to work in a full-time capacity.

I continued to apply for all kinds of jobs and would get some interviews, but never considered for employment. I didn't realize until later that it's not what you know, it's who you know. Also, it's not what you did, it's how you portray what you did. An individual with little job experience can make him/her appear as a rock star with the proper placement of buzzwords and formatting within their resume. Because I did not have the resume writing skill to sell my own accomplishments, I was never able to get the job that I felt I deserved based on my aptitude and skill.

I took classes every semester as often as I could to make up the loss of income from not having a job.....or better yet, not having a career. During my second year of graduate school, still desperate for a job, but not giving the opportunity I wanted, I lowered my standards for the experience and the income. I reached out to an employment specialist who placed me in contact with a security company. Fortunately, they hired me very quickly and gave me a security supervisor job. My security staff consisted of 12 officers and it paid me $14 an hour.

I was a combat veteran with management experience and 3 college degrees, but my job was a security supervisor. Humble pie always tastes great. Plus, the security job gave me enough leverage to focus more on my learning. But the security job was in a socially disadvantaged building which housed low-income, substance abuse, and mental health residents who had many dangerous ties to the community. The police department made regular trips to our building in response to drugs, overdoses, & mental disturbances.

Nevertheless, my focus was on completing the last year of my master degree. With very little prospect in New York City for me and my family, I started to look back in Georgia for employment. I was thankfully employed as a Community Supervision Officer in March of 2016. I left NYC and returned to my home and family in Valdosta Georgia. Thankfully, I was able to work with my professors to take my course remotely while I trained at the Officer Academy. In June of 2016, I graduated with both my Master's Degree and my Peace Officer Certification in Georgia. I loved being a Community Supervision Officer, but I realized that law enforcement was not meant for me throughout my time spent as a Community Supervision Officer. I am considerably too nice for the Law Enforcement community. I did not fear my community at all and wanted to help them obey the law. Contrary to other officers,

I would watch the fear and mistrust in the eyes of law enforcement officers everyday they walked and talked to the community. Additionally, I've watched black men and women receive harsher sentences than their white counterparts in a court of law. I treated all the men and women I supervised equally at all times and held no bias towards them. Meaning, I tried my hardest to keep them out of jail by being their positive outlook on life, but I also laid the hammer when I legally had to. I would watch the judges give my black probationer 9 months in prison (at my request), and give no prison time to my white probationer (against my request). Both individuals violated their terms and deserved to be sent to a drug rehab center in prison that was 9 months long, and both were given different sentences for the same violation. Why???

These constant actions by judges broke me and I lost faith that this system is fair to everyone; I would countlessly watch the racial disparity between sentences in the southern regions of Georgia. I lasted for 18 months before I left law enforcement with the intent of never applying for such a position again in the future. It's just not for me. I have no fear of my community that I served, which was foreign to the police officer. I enjoyed talking to people and I didn't have in the back of my mind the dangers of dying on the job. I figured if I died talking to someone or chasing someone down, then the officers behind me knew they could do what they need with a clear conscience. None of these traits is commensurate with the fearful nature of being a law enforcement individual. I've never been around so many scared people in all my life. Not to say that there is no bravery among the police force because there is. But officers assume the worst will happen every day they work and live their lives in fear that today will be the day.

The year is now 2018 and I've accepted a full-time position with the Community College of the Air Force for one year. This was another job that was just meant to fill up the time until I found my perfect career. After separating from active duty, I chose a career in Emergency Management as it would best compliment my skills. But four years later, I have no idea what the fuck I am doing. I wanted and applied for Emergency Management jobs all the time and never got picked up because of my experience or the way my resume is written. Not to mention, my interviewing skills were not great at all. I never applied common techniques like S.A.R. (Situation, Action, Result) to my answers. Even though I had the experience and the lessons learned to do so, it was difficult for me to pick up the mechanics of performing well at an interview. So I turned to YouTube and blogs over the internet to gain insight on what I was doing wrong and worked hard to correct it.

I would go to sleep and wake up asking "what the fuck am I doing here?" I'm not on the path I set for myself and I'm veering farther away from it with every day that passes. I was confused and overall lost. I cried many nights and fell into deep depressive states because my future was uncertain. I have a family to care for and I cannot obtain a career that is in-line with my goals in the same place my family lives. My wife and children were in our house in Valdosta GA, and I worked in Montgomery Alabama and traveled home on the weekend. I worked in a position where an Associate's Degree was needed, and had a Master Degree. Depression hit me hard as I started to blame the color of my skin, the people around me, not being tough enough, not having the attitude that fit the crowd, my level of intelligence....everything was up for grabs.

I was a failure and couldn't get out of my funk, no matter what anyone told me. My outlook on the year's end was dark and forever unclear. I was only assigned to the Alabama assignment for 1 year. What will I do after that? I'm still applying for jobs and receiving 100% rejections. I later learned (through investigation) that previous supervisors were providing employers with false information about me and defaming my character in secret, assuming I would never find out (freedom of information act request fixed that). I felt like the world hated me and no matter what I did, I couldn't get out from under this rock of shame. With the life difficulty I kept experiencing, I enrolled myself in therapy so I wouldn't hurt myself or others. I'm here to tell you, I'm a veteran, I live in the south, I owned several guns.....I came damn close to hurting myself because of the overwhelming depression and state of worthlessness. Military service came with Post Traumatic Stress (PTS) which clouded my decision making process because I couldn't solve my problems with violence, and boy did I want to. For everyone who stood in my way and placed barriers in front of me, I wanted to hurt or destroy. For those who would take me away from the prosperity of life and being with my family, I wanted to hurt them severely. PTS kept me angry and wanting to solve my problems with violence of action because that's what I had been used to.

Destroying obstacles placed in front of me in order to accomplish the mission. I needed to speak to someone immediately and used the services provided by the mental health offices (on and off base). Most of my sessions were filled with me being angry at what has happened to me and how I am not successful. I never cried during a session, but I came there angry and left less angry. But all good things are temporary and will end eventually. Since the position I was in was counted as active duty service, I was due to separate again in August, 2019. What would I do differently? I still had no pending jobs waiting for me that will help me get back to my family and fulfill my career aspirations. I needed income, I wanted to be with my family after years of being apart for deployments, college, and training. What can I do? I got it, I'll start a business and run it from my house so that I can be with my family as long and as much as possible. What could go wrong? I took a deep look at my priorities and noticed for years they have been out of place with where they should be.

My wife and children were missing out on the best years we could have together because I was too consumed with career structure and placement. It is important to choose a career that you love, but it is also important that the career loves you back. Just like in a loving relationship, there is compromise and constant communication between both parties. For years I had become stuck in careers that I enjoyed, but the career, the people, the location did not love me back. I would place my everything into these jobs and professions, and I received more negative outcomes from it. It was time to place me and my happiness first above all else.

I decided to become a Personal Fitness trainer that would operate business from my home. I had already invested into home gym equipment, but what if I converted my garage into an actual gym space. Space for those who enjoyed working out, but wanted the privacy of personal training away from the crowds of the people. I sought out to become the best and only home fitness space in Valdosta GA. I had never owned a business, but I was making a little money from Affiliate Marketing using my fitness website and my YouTube videos.

I focused primarily on my infrastructure as I needed more equipment, but more equipment meant I needed more money. And I was about to be unemployed after my military orders ended. I wasn't generating enough money to sustain the starter cost for a home gym upgrade....so what could I do? Running a business is risky because you never know how it will go. It might do great.....but it might not go anywhere. I knew I had to take a risk so...I decided to use my home as a source of capital by refinancing my mortgage.

The decision to buy a home was to provide my family stability and ownership for our children to one day inherited to build generational wealth. My home currently had about $35K in equity and I decided to refinance it to consolidate and pay off my credit card debt and liquidate about $15K to purchase new equipment. This would raise my mortgage by $200 per month which at the time (with probable income) was still affordable. Once I received the cash from the refinance, I invested in paint, flooring, safety measures, and a ton of new equipment for both strength training and functional training. I also budgeted for marketing and equipment giveaways for those who participated during my marketing campaign.

I was overly confident and excited to start my business that would keep me home with my family and allow me to make the income I needed to be successful. I was September 2018 and I decided I would fully launch for clients on October 1st 2018 (after 9 months of planning). It took me a total of 2 months to build the gym for client use, obtain my certifications, create my Personal Training website which was easy to make. I was ready, and started producing leads via Facebook and google ads. But I surely learned that simply having a lead does not guarantee sales as I did not have a closer mentality. The art of sales is just that, an Art. This was an art form I did not excel at, which ultimately cost me business opportunities and customers. Nevertheless, I needed my own business as a means for me to be home with my family. Transitioning does not only mean from career to career, but to transition back to being a part of my family on a full-time basis.

Launch day came on 1 October. I officially opened for business and am awaiting my first client. But the clients never came. I figured I would just wait a while, they will show up eventually through the week, throughout the months, throughout the quarter. I patiently responded to leads and reached out to prospective clients telling them I am ready for business with brand new equipment, workout plans and various payment options that are affordable for the consumer compared to the market. A week pass and no clients. 2 weeks pass, no clients. A month went by, no clients. This trend continued throughout all my efforts which caused me to close my business and sell off all my equipment in order to keep my bills paid and my family fed.

Taking the risk to start and halt my business was a decision that I made knowing the risk would be great. I use the word halt because I never truly stop running my business. I have simply re-engineered it using the lessons I've learned from the failures of the past. Today, I still hold my Personal Training certification and my websites are still 100% operational allowing me to take on clients as needed. I have registered my business in the State of New York as I have received a job opportunity to work as an Emergency Manager for a hospital system in the city. This was a great opportunity because I have been unemployed for 6 months with zero income. My mortgage was behind and it was very difficult to maintain a normal sense of living for me and my family. My transition from the military, to businessman, to unemployed, to working in a career in which all my skills have culminated towards. Things are starting to look upward. And thank goodness because I was becoming wary from all the lessons I was forced to learn during my transition.

Foxtrot Transition

Always have a plan for the plan because all your plans will fail. No matter how confident you are of your chances of landing that perfect job in the perfect place, actively plan as if it will fail. This is not to discourage the prospect of success in your life, but to maintain a readiness posture for unforeseen circumstances. Be confident in nothing else but your ability to plan for the next event when the current one fails. Your duty when you transition in any aspect of your life is to be ready for all hell to break loose. Be ready for the fight that you know is coming your way.

Transition Seven:

From Start to Finish - <u>Knowing when you've won.</u>

The most important lesson you will have to teach yourself when transitioning from worker to student, from military to civilian, from civilian to elected official, etc., is to realize when you have accomplished the goal that was set by your previous self. Knowing exactly what you want will make the difference in your transition going smoothly or never coming to fruition. My transition from the beginning to the end took almost 18 years. 18 years for me to make the income I knew I deserved. 18 Years for me to obtain the level of education I craved. And 18 years for me to finally be in the career I've dreamed of. Getting to this point in my life is not isolated to my experience, but it is shared through millions of people all over who don't know when to ask "is this enough?" Knowing when you have completed your task in life will be different for everyone. What ruins the chance at finally meeting your objective for transitioning is knowing when to quit.

For myself, the time came in 2020 during the Coronavirus pandemic. My military service was about to end in June of 2020 and at the time, from Aug 2019 - March 2020, I was the owner of a non-successful fitness business. I had so many hopes for my business to soar and make the money I wanted to make. Scratch that, the money I needed to make. With zero clients who were willing to pay for my services, I had to do what I could in order to pay my bills and keep my family protected. This meant refinancing my home in order to pay for my start-up cost. It also meant selling all my fitness equipment to people all over the county via Facebook marketplace and online ads once the business ultimately failed. I started my business in October 2019, and went broke by January 2020. I started the New Year with debt and zero income to take care of my family. I needed to find the next career that would give me the opportunity to be the leader I was and to somehow, take care of my family. After my last piece of my fitness equipment was sold,

I made enough money to keep the lights on for 2 more months. In February 2020 I began to contemplate returning back to school. Because I was able to use the last 6 months of my GI Bill to help me pay for school and to pay for my living expenses. Naturally I would attend school in New York City because of the high housing allowance, and because my family still lives there (giving me a place to stay). While I was looking for which program I wanted to attend, I remembered my passion for Emergency Management and how until this moment, I had been simply performing jobs that were opportunistic. My military career was an opportunity to serve my country after 9/11 (opportunistic).

My short career in Probation Parole operations in Georgia gave me the opportunity to work in Valdosta (opportunistic). My yearlong tour working at the Community College of the

Air Force gave my family income to avoid unemployment for one year (opportunistic). With all these randomized opportunities that presented to me, it was clear that I was just working any job that came my way. Once my military goal of participating in combat was fulfilled, I no longer desired to stay in the military. I had served my county and almost died on many occasions in doing so.

What was next for me? Emergency Management was what I had been studying during my Master's degree program in 2014. I enjoyed the analytical tact it took in order to prepare large organizations and even cities for emergencies. I had not known it at the time, but I missed the joy I had from learning & participating in emergency responses. I was placed on this planet to help and protect others and without realizing, I already had been. It was time to return to what I was born to do, become an Emergency Manager. But how do I go about it and what companies will have me?

It was no secret I had applied to Emergency Management jobs in the past and have had some interviews but no offers. It was time to use what went right and not use what went wrong during the interview process. I spend days creating canned scripts that answered the most asked question at my interviews. Also, I placed all my accolades and accomplishments on paper for me to readily review and refer to during an interview. I also learned that I must focus my objective as finite as possible. Not only was pursuing my career in emergency management, but I was re-enrolling back in school to learn more about the U.S. healthcare system as a future healthcare manager. With this level of education (additionally to my other degrees and credentials), I will be the most marketable emergency management specialist within the healthcare system.

The stage was set for me to win the position and to obtain the last (truly last) bit of education I can obtain while leveraging my veteran benefits. I returned to NYC in March of 2020 with the hope of re-inventing my fitness business with the backdrop of NYC. But then, COVID-19 started to spread and took hold of the city. Fortunately, within two days of me being back in NY, I received two job offers. One was from a Consulting firm (Hagerty Consulting) with a start date of the following week. Another, from The Mount Sinai Hospital (tentative upon final approval).

While I conducted my Mount Sinai interview over the phone in the rain outside my father's apartment building, it was 100% worth it. Although I was able to start the job working with the consulting firm, I did finally receive a job offer from Mount Sinai to work for them one week after I started to work for the consulting firm. Working in Consulting was a fast learning experience working directly for the logistics operations of the NYC Emergency Management. Once I accepted the Mount Sinai position, I politely informed my Human Resource contact at Hagerty that I will be leaving for a different opportunity. At this point, Hagerty had offered me a full-time position (as I was working for them on a probationary basis) due to my quality of work within that week. I declined based on the offered salary, but they countered with an additionally 10,000 dollars. I still declined and was very honored and humbled by the experience. At this point, my brain and soul started to feel as if my life plans were finally coming together. Is this it....what i've waited for? Are my days of trying, crying, worrying, and doubting myself are over? Did I win? Finally, have I won the battle of life and the struggles to transition?

Where would I have been had I not decided to join the Air Force all those years ago. I had no idea where my life was heading as a teenager from the Bronx whose only skill was playing the saxophone. I mean, I went to high school to learn music, with no ambition or desire to become a musician professionally. What was I thinking? I had no vision or direction as to what I wanted for myself. All I worried about when I was a young boy growing up in New York City was having fun, looking fly, and finding girls to hopefully one day have sex with. My views were totally limited and so were my options. In some way shape or form, September 11th changed my life in a positive direction when the entire country was suffering from the sheer horror of that event.

What's important to know is that ending your transition from one place to the next place is a choice. We chose to stop wanting, we chose to stop looking, we chose to settle in the place that makes us most comfortable. My comfortable place was hard to find because I was the roadblock that prevented me from moving forward. I didn't know when to start and most importantly, when to stop. It was not a natural occurrence for me to slow down and to not search, search, and search for the next opportunity. Indeed, that's all I've been used to was the high operational tempo that demanded constant repetition leading to perfection. No one was harder on my professional skill and competencies than myself. Never feeling like I was good enough or simply enough for others to accept me was a daily battle that raged internally. This came from the constant undermining from members in my Air Force unit who, for some fucking reason, referred to me as if I was stupid. In fact, there were a few of my squadron members who would tell people I was the dumbest person in the unit.

This was without a doubt one of my lowest points in my career because it made me feel like the world will never accept an educated black man. No matter what we did, or how much education we obtained, if we (black men) were not like the majority of our colleges (who were mostly white), I was questioned about everything I did. Fortunately, I didn't give a fuck about any of that and I knew what my worth was. It didn't matter what anyone thought about me, I knew I was special, intelligent, kind, and deserved to have a seat at the table. My quest for acceptance within the military and within the civilian sector was based on my need for more knowledge. The need for acceptance from others forced me to always produce the best quality product (shooting, running, systems understanding, Emergency Management principles). I wanted to be the best.....so it happened. When you've become your best self, your search will end. You will have met your mark and achieved your goals. Because you matter, you are worth it, you are enough. Finally realizing you CAN stop running the rat race means you've accepted your place in this world.

Be proud of yourself and your accomplishments. Transitioning only ends when you've learned to accept your place in this world. Enjoy the journey and never shy away from a tough lesson that can only be taught by never missing a day in life.

The Final Transition

Applying when & how to better your life.

Learn from the mistakes of others and create your own path.

Make a plan, then plan for it to fail!

There is no surprise that shocks the human soul more than unanticipated failure. We as a culture have built a path for success and assume that success is inevitable. Your mission when it's time to transition in any aspect of your life is to have a plan, respect the plan, follow the plan, & know that your plan will fail. There is a saying that failure is not an option, but it most certainly is. You will fail at most things in life, but failure breeds intelligence. Failure makes us stronger, and failure ultimately creates resilience. We are not a spoiled culture of privileged people who have a trust fund to fall back on. Human nature is built for tough times and resilience. Acceptance of that truth will create an environment where your ability to conform and adjust will be strengthened. Your transition will at times be the toughest event you may endure in your life. Be ready for it by eliminating the naive notion that failure is not an option. That is a nonsensical saying meant for people who do not have the analytical will to push through adversity. You....we.... are not those folks. We plan for failure, not because we are weak, but because we are strong enough to understand that the game never ends. Keep playing, even when you've lost.

Never sell yourself short, but learn how to sell yourself!

Being your own cheerleader is not easy. When you can't cheer yourself on, find honest friends or family who will tell you your best and worst qualities and do me a favor.......listen without questions. You must be able to listen to the harsh criticism given to you by the people you respect as well as the people you do not. You will always have to just shut the fuck up and simply listen to the words of everyone else who is not you. Take in all that is said, good or bad about you and turn it into cash, money, bullets on your resume, or multiple job offers. Keep this in mind, you know how much you're worth. If you know you are worth a certain amount of money, do not accept anything less when looking for the perfect salary. Not every job that pays well is for you. Learn to say no when appropriate and when you know saying yes will hurt you.

Leave those who are not about your success behind, and never look back!

There are so many toxic people in this world who do not deserve your space. Tell them to kick rocks early and be secure that you never needed them in the first place. You can easily spot these individuals or organizations who will keep you from being the person or professional you want to be. For the organization, you may be debating leaving it behind, remembering the times you were denied for that training event, that promotion, that pay raise, or the invitation to accept more responsibility. Personally, I always wanted to be an Officer in the United States Air Force. I spent 18 years as an Airman in our great military and when I accomplished my bachelor's degree in 2013, I opted to take the test to become an Officer called the AFOQT. I never doubted my level of intelligence or my ability to lead, but when I took the test and didn't obtain the minimum score to be competitive, it was hard to accept. Some things just aren't meant for you. The day I accepted I won't be an Officer in the Air Force, I focused on where my career was meant to be....and it wasn't as an Air Force Officer, but as an Emergency Management Director. Don't spend your life trying to put a square into a circular slot. Be proud to be a square, be proud to be different. Be proud to be unique among your peers. You've seen your organization or toxic friends reject you in subtle ways. THEY DON'T WANT YOU....but YOU want you more than everyone else. The signs are different and loud as hell if you tune all the bullshit out listen closely.

It's ok to cry, it's never ok to quit!

There is no paragraph of wisdom needed for this. Take time for yourself and cry every once in a while. So what....cry when you are down...cry when things don't go your way......cry when you are close to giving up.

But never ever EVER fucking quit on yourself or those who depend on you. It is never ok to quit. You quit, and you will NEVER be the greatness you are meant to be.

Never stop learning, destroy the idle mind!

Learning never stops when you become an adult with a plan. As we age, we assume there is nothing else we need to formally learn in a controlled setting. You would be wrong. The sooner you can accept that you will never be as smart as you think, the smarter you will become. You will always strive to learn more, sign up for another class. Volunteer to instructor others on the skill you have mastered. Do not let your mind become idle due to not acting or doing. The mind is complex and capable of achieving greatness. If you see a class you can take that will better your career options...take it. Take that dance class with your special loved one. Hire a fitness professional to give you the best workout plan of your life. Go back to school and earn that degree that will increase your career chances for success. Don't just obtain a degree in underwater basket weaving that does nothing to make you better at making the world a better place. It's about the substance of what you chose to learn...not just having a piece of paper.

Ask for feedback often, but make your own decisions!

Be the person that demands your peers and supervisors share their thoughts about your performance. I have been fortunate to have great friends in my life who were always willing to share exactly what I did right and what I suck at. Find your person who will give you the honesty and respect you deserve. You will thank that person everyday of your life during your transitions from amateur to professional. There is no better report card than the one from close friends or supervisors who want to see you succeed. There are so few people in the world who have the balls to tell you how much you need to improve, but stick by your side. The people who matter the most to your life are the ones that will stick around when the going gets tough. But understand this…...make your own decision. Even when you make a mistake and make the wrong decision, be proud of the decision you made. Nothing happens in a bubble and if you are smart and listen to the internal thoughts screaming at you...learning will occur. Every action you take is connected with the actions you haven't thought of yet. Stick by your decisions, support your success and your failures. Make a decision, even if it's the wrong one.

Volunteer for everything! Go and do what others won't.

Be the first one through the door and accept the risk that comes with that burden. Be the one that everyone can depend on, even when they don't thank you for it. Your thank you will come with the experience you gain from being everywhere that no one else wanted to go. Go where those do not dare, and ask again and again to send me. Be the one that is called upon to complete the task that only you can complete. Volunteer for everything no matter what.

Thank you for spending your time with me and allowing me to share my story. This memoir is dedicated to my wife and children who have always been there for me throughout all my transitions. Without them and their support, there is no way I could've made it this far in my journey.

Thank you Katherine, my handsome Jaden & and my beautiful Kayle.

I love you all with all of me.

William C. Gonzalez

Made in the USA
Monee, IL
22 November 2021

82710984R00085